A HOME COURSE IN
NUTRITION

Books by
ERIC F. W. POWELL

A HOME COURSE IN NUTRITION

by
Eric F. W. Powell
Ph.D., N.D

HEALTH SCIENCE PRESS
Bradford   Holsworthy
Devon

ISBN 0 85032158 1

Printed in Great Britain by
Clarke, Doble & Brendon Limited
Plymouth & London

CONTENTS

FOREWORD

These lessons in nutrition are intended as a helpful and practical guide to proper feeding, and cover the whole of the necessary matters connected with the subject. Food for the mind has not been neglected.

Some of the subjects dealt with are so important that no apology is made for their repetition.

Readers who carry out the suggestions made to the best of their ability will add greatly to life and happiness. Read and apply, and results are assured.

Read the lessons again and again. To read and not put the lessons into practice is a waste of time.

Eric F. Powell. Ph.D., N.D.

ABOUT NUTRITION

LESSON 1

It is said that nutrition is the physical basis of life, and that we are what we eat. This is a part truth, for it is not so much what we eat as what we assimilate that does us good – or ill as the case may be. Physical health results from the perfect assimilation of natural, properly grown foods, although, as will be discussed later in this course, health also depends on positive thinking and sane living.

Many people live to eat, when one should eat to live. As the Bible says, with some 'their god is in their bellies'. On the other hand 'fadding' over foods can be as bad as wrong feeding. The writer has contacted scores of diet fads who after fussing over their diet for many years are just as ill as they were before they started on their pet theories. It is not necessary to be a food faddist, and in most cases the application of common sense is all that is necessary to attain and maintain a goodly measure of radiant well being. To be obsessed with ideas about food leads to introspection, and introspection is a disease of itself. Health tends to come to those who do not worry about it. On the other hand living can be a joy when one plays the game of life according to the rules. Live in order to live! The mind obsessed with the self most of the time is never healthy. Decide what is sensible, carry it out in daily living and forget the self.

The blood is the life, and what we eat to a very large extent determines the nature of the blood and its circulation throughout the system. The osteopaths say that health is the result of perfect circulation, and to a large extent they are right. It must be kept in mind that the perfect circulation of good, chemically balanced blood depends on clean, natural food, thorough mastication, daily exercise (even if only in walking and physical games), the intake of oxygen, restful sleep and a happy, hopeful disposition. All these matters will be dealt with in this course.

Pioneers of the past settling in new countries, were a hardy lot of people. Why were they so healthy? The answer is that they fed on foods grown naturally in good soil — soil not contaminated by chemicals or polluted in any fashion, and not exhausted by the continuous growing of crops. Also these people had plenty of fresh air and physical exercise. They were too busy to have time to think about themselves. Laziness of mind or body leads to functional inactivity when everything becomes sluggish and unhealthy. There is nothing more still than a corpse. Life is activity! Stagnation is death!

What is pain? It is nature's warning that something is wrong. To banish the pain with drugs does not remove the reason why the pain manifested. Indeed in many instances the drug administered could even add to the cause. The orthodox system of medicine deals mainly with effects and not with causes. In like manner tranquillizing drugs administered to relieve pain, banish headaches and induce sleep, never deal with basic causes. To render the nerves senseless by means of drugs means that nature can no longer give the warning signal. It has to be admitted that in some cases pain relief is most important, but at the same time steps should be taken to diagnose the reason or reasons why pain is present.

Orthodox concoctions which usually consist of crude minerals, used for giving ease to sufferers from indigestion never deal with the reasons why the indigestion or stomach

10

pain is present. The medicine administered may deal with an existing acid condition and thereby give relief, but the cause of the acidity is constitutional and if the reasons for the acidity are not eliminated the trouble will return. In most instances the sufferer has to rely more and more on the prescribed medicine for relief.

The organs of digestion, like all other organs, consist mainly of muscle. Healthy muscles mean healthy organs, and a healthy organ is never in distress. To improve a muscle it has to be exercised and well nourished. Taking drugs to perform the work intended to be done by a muscular organ means that that organ has less to do and the muscles become weaker and weaker. As muscles and organs depend on the blood for nourishment cure depends on the circulation of good blood in the affected tissues, and this can only be accomplished by eating and well masticating pure food, by a better intake of oxygen and taking remedial exercise to strengthen the parts. Remember that a healthy organ cannot be diseased and is, therefore, free from pain. Sane dieting alone may cure in some instances although usually attention has to be paid to other matters.

Authorities agree that the body is a self-healing mechanism if the necessary body building and healing elements are present in the blood. A cut finger is not healed by the ointment applied, but by the blood. And it is the same with disorders present within the organism — always the blood is the healer. Some may suggest that in a diseased state the system has been invaded by germs. True, disease germs are present in a diseased organ, but what are they and why are they there?

Where filth is present so are the flies. It may be said that disease germs are scavengers: they feed on diseased products and are present because morbid matter is in the affected organ or tissues. R. Virchow, one of the sponsors of the germ theory, wrote: 'If I could live my life over again, I would devote it to proving that germs seek their natural habitat — diseased tissue — rather than being the cause of the diseased tissue; e.g. mosquitos seek the stagnant water, but do not cause the pool to become stagnant.' Fear of germs and of invasions from without may kill twenty people while the disease itself may kill only one. If the germ theory were founded on real facts the earth would soon be wiped clean of all living things. Some of the leading lights in the orthodox system of medicine have admitted that too much attention has been paid to germs and not nearly enough to the host of the germs.

The writer has met orthodox doctors who do not like administering some of the modern drugs, but in the circumstances feel that they have to do so. How often have drugs produced dangerous side effects which in some instances were worse than the disorder for which they were given! Some doctors turn to homoeopathy, a system which is harmless and based on natural law. The homoeopath treats the person rather than the disease. The ancient school of herbal medicine achieved much and a good herbalist can often do what the orthodox practitioner cannot, for the medicines the herbalist employs are organic, non-poisonous and do not produce other disorders. Neither is there any record of a herbalist or homoeopath producing deformed babies!

Yet the powers that be seem to be doing their best to get rid of herbalists and are restricting the supply of homoeopathic medicines to practitioners who are not orthodox trained doctors. It is a strange world and inverted reasoning seems to be the order of the day.

The art of surgery has attained great heights, and on occasions natural healers have to recommend surgery. Yet we all have to admit that surgery (except in cases of accidents) is an admission that medicine has failed. When a doctor cannot accomplish anything it is a case of sending the sufferer to a surgeon, and in the opinion of many natural healers surgery is totally unnecessary in quite a number of cases. We have even known of young women being sent to hospital to have a cystic ovary removed, and the surgeon had taken out the other healthy ovary as well, this making motherhood impossible. This is not surgery but scientific butchery. Many women have their breasts removed and are mutilated as a

12

result, when homoeopathy or natural therapy could have prevented it. Tonsils have been removed when the operation was unnecessary, but not to the extent as formerly, for doctors now face the fact that tonsils are eliminative organs and are in the body for a purpose. The same with the appendix. Before the reign of Edward VII appendicitis was regarded as old-fashioned tummy-ache and no more dangerous. Then surgical removal came into fashion and thousands of people lost an appendix for no other reason than to satisfy the surgeon by removing an 'unwanted' organ. The appendix also, is a detoxicating organ and serves a useful purpose. The reason why tonsils or an appendix became inflamed or septic seems to have been neglected. Of course there are cases when the removal of a very diseased organ is essential to save life, but such cases are in a minority.

So often do we hear that the operation was successful, but the patient died.

Always the natural healer will seek to deal with the cause and treat the toxic individual as a whole. All diseased glands and organs are a result of wrong living and impure blood.

These remarks must not be taken as an attack on orthodox doctors. The medical profession consists of highly skilled and dedicated men and women. Some wear themselves out in doing their best to help suffering humanity. They place themselves at anybody's service day and night and a good doctor is capable of bringing much help and comfort to the sick. It is the system of medicine that is wrong. The orthodox theory is that in order to cure one disease it is necessary to create another. It is called 'allopathy', which means 'another disease or pain'. Evil cannot be destroyed with evil, but good can overcome evil and nature's methods are the best. Healing in harmony with nature's laws must be right.

When one has disturbing symptoms or is feeling really ill it is wise to have the condition diagnosed. Never mess about with the so-called 'wonder cures' for if the actual nature of the trouble is not discovered deterioration may take place. Some naturists have so neglected this matter that they have departed this life long before they should have done when timely professional advice would have cleared the disturbance. Because a doctor is orthodox that does not mean that he is foolish. The expert diagnosis of a highly trained man or woman is so often of great importance. One may disagree with the orthodox theory of treatment, but the wholesale condemnation of orthodox doctors can be a grave mistake. The writer has known many doctors, both orthodox and those who have abandoned the orthodox theory, and on the whole found them to be conscientious and dedicated people. One has to agree that there are many unorthodox practitioners who have been badly trained and fall short when it comes to accuracy in diagnosis. The leading nature cure establishments know this and are taking steps to have all students very thoroughly trained.

The best of treatments can prove fruitless if the original diagnosis is in error. We are concerned with prevention rather than cure, and a healthy organism cannot become diseased. Note the word itself: '*dis*-ease' − a lack of ease or harmony within the system. We are not so much concerned with various forms of healing in these writings as with disease prevention, and in this matter diet is of vital importance. Also it is possible not only to ward off disease but to deal effectively with many disturbed conditions already existing in the organism; also to promote a long, useful and a happy life.

Some practitioners maintain that food should be our only medicines. We cannot agree with this; in any case not with the foods provided today. Soil and vegetation are all being slowly poisoned by the employment of chemical fertilisers and poisonous sprays. Even the insects and birds are being destroyed as a result of this practice. But properly grown foods are medicinal and can play a vital part in restoring health to poorly-functioning organs. Many wild herbs have escaped chemical contamination, and it must be remembered that our cultivated vegetables were originally wild herbs. There are those who object to the use of herbs and rely on cultivated vegetables only. This is sheer stupidity in these times. Wild herbs contain more vitamins and essential organised minerals than the over-cultivated, chemically treated

14

produce of the shops. If one can grow one's own vegetables according to natural law so much the better, although some farmers grow crops correctly and avoid chemicalisation in any of its dangerous forms. The demand for such crops is growing.

To keep to the Levitic laws pertaining to soil treatment is wise. We should return to the earth what comes from it as nature does herself. The garden soil should be dressed with compost and animal excreta. To do this means healthy, disease-free and better tasting crops.

Compost grown vegetables may cost a little more, but at least to feed on such means that one is being properly nourished and not poisoned. Also, one requires less pure food than one does of the 'treated' variety, so the cost is not any more in the end. A small plateful of clean food well masticated will accomplish far more good than a large plateful of the wrong food improperly chewed. It is not what one eats so much as what one assimilates. There is much medicinal value as well as real nourishment in pure food well masticated.

A young man who was a pronounced neurasthenic, had lost all his hair and was very much depleted, was restored to full health by taking a short fast followed by a natural diet. He received no other treatment or medication; and doctors had given him up. His basic trouble was faulty nutrition and very poor assimilative powers. He soon grew a healthy crop of hair.

Before dealing with dieting and the value of foods it is necessary that mastication be discussed. No matter how good a food may be, the full value will not be obtained unless it is well masticated — that is what teeth are for, and they are in the mouth and not in the stomach. Many weakly people have been restored to good health by doing nothing more than thoroughly masticating their food. One man named Fletcher did so much good by teaching the sick to masticate well that the process had been termed 'Fletcherisation'. This man claims that he first cured himself after being literally sentenced to death by the doctors, by chewing every mouthful of food to a pulp before swallowing. The great Gladstone learned to masticate his food and lived a very long and useful life. He

15

claimed that he chewed food thirty times before swallowing.

The mouth may be said to be the house of preparation in which the food is chemically dealt with by the saliva, by the action of chewing. The saliva is a biochemical compound which helps to convert starches into natural sugar. It is able to deal with acid in the food and does much to prevent acidity in the stomach. When the food is not thoroughly masticated it is not ready for later processes of digestive assimilation, and when such food enters the stomach it tends to cause a toxic condition and sets up indigestion. Food thus badly prepared enters the intestines in a condition not fit for absorption and cannot produce pure blood. The result of this is a whole batch of disorders such as arthritis, rheumatism, catarrh, auto-toxaemia (self-poisoning), constipation, inflammations, general debility and scores of other conditions. Every organ in the body can suffer as a result of incomplete mastication.

It is said that during periods of famine certain African peoples will partake of foods normally regarded as being poisonous, and they have learned that by thoroughly masticating such foods the undesirable ingredients are rendered harmless and edible. Such is the value of mastication that even the wrong food can be made to contribute to physical health and vitality. It follows, therefore, that the very first thing to learn in dietetics is how to eat. The valuable advice given in these pages will not accomplish what is intended unless this first essential has been learned and put into practice.

Think of the domestic cow who supplies us with an abundance of milk which contains all the nutrients essential to growth and life. This animal not only chews very thoroughly, but even regurgitates to give the food another going over in her mouth. She thus obtains every atom of nourishment — even from grass.

So much has been written about dietetics, calories, vitamins and the so-called 'wonder foods' that people are confused. Indeed, it could well be that the more people read about the subject the less they know about it. The reader is advised to

16

forget about vitamins, calories, test tube experiments, the results of animal experimentation and everything else along those lines and apply common sense. Always we have to deal with the individual human being and, unlike sheep, we tend to differ.

A food may appear to look exceptionally good, but may not suit the individual. It is useless advising a person to eat raw food if he or she is incapable of digesting it, or to advise the very thin to eat more in order to put on weight. It has been truthfully said that more people dig their graves with their teeth than die from famine. As a rule those suffering from obesity require more fresh fruit than the thin, who need more green leafy vegetables.

One of the great errors has been to advise people who are ill to eat in order to keep up their strength. When ill or much depressed, food, especially heavy meals, should be avoided. Man is the only animal who eats when he is ill. The animals obey an inborn instinct and avoid all food when they are ill. In the wild state they usually manage to get well without the attention of vets or kindly-disposed human interference.

Should you find that a certain food does not agree with you, then shun such a food, even if it has been advised by a doctor or dietetic expert.

Jesus of Nazareth indicated that what comes out of one's mouth is more destructive than what goes into it. His remarks show that wrong thoughts, especially when expressed in words, have a poisoning effect, while the organs of digestion are designed to deal with what goes into the mouth. He did, however, advise people to keep to the Mosaic and Levitical laws respecting diet. All that is wise and helpful in human living is based on these laws from the treatment of the soil to human conduct.

When one is mentally upset or angry one should not eat, for food taken in such circumstances tends to turn poisonous. On the other hand happiness and mirth at the table aid digestion and promote assimilation. There is much in the almost forgotten habit of saying grace before meals: it indicates a thankful state of mind and a grateful mind does much to prepare for the process of digestion.

Never engage in other persuits when eating, but keep the mind on eating and enjoying the food. When one is really hungry one can eat the simplest of foods and enjoy what is eaten. There are different theories regarding times for meals. The writer's experience suggests that meal times should be arranged according to occupation. Also, it is better to eat a little several times a day than to gorge on one or two enormous meals, which overload the stomach and causes upset with gas accumulation. This does not mean that one has to 'nibble' all through the day, for as a rule one who is constantly nibbling will, in addition, partake of the usual large meals at the usual hours.

Dr. George Starr White, one of the most brilliant physicians of our age, gives the following diet hints. The good doctor was so concerned with the erronous habit of thought and human values that he had a large arch over the entrance to his residence with the word 'think' in large letters. He maintained that most people in our time have forgotten how to think and that we have been degraded by the teachings of modern pseudo science. He says:

Do not eat unless hungry.

Do not eat when you are ill or feeling out of sorts.

Do not eat more than enough to satisfy hunger.

Do not eat rapidly, for if you do you cannot tell whether you have eaten enough or too much.

Do not forget that every mouthful of food in excess of your requirements acts as a poison to the system.

Do not eat fruit with starches or unnatural sweets.

Do not eat a variety of foods at one meal. The nearer you can get to one class of food at a meal the better.

Do not wash your food down. Eat it as nearly dry as possible.

Do not forget that the first act of digestion is putting the food into the mouth, and the next is thoroughly masticating it.

Do not forget that time spent in chewing food is time well spent.

Do not eat any food that you do not like. As you improve in health you will find that you will like any natural food. Dis-

18

liking certain foods is a sure indication that your digestive apparatus is out of order.

Do not eat or drink anything, unless as a remedy, within three hours before retiring.

Do not judge as to whether food has agreed with you or not until three or four hours after having eaten it.

Do not eat anything that produces a feeling of fullness in the stomach or abdomen. The full feeling is caused by fermentation, which produces alcohol and gas.

Do not eat pickled foods of any kind.

Do not take vinegar. Lemon juice will take the place of vinegars on all greens, but should never be taken at the same meal with starches or unnatural sweets.

Do not eat any kind of fats as they are not only unnecessary, but also have a great tendency to disturb the functions of the liver.

Do not eat anything you fear will hurt you — remember that fear is the worst disease known to humans.

Do not eat salt, pepper or any other condiments.

Do not eat any fried foods.

Do not eat anything made of denatured (white) flour.

Do not eat any refined sugar or anything in which it is used. Honey is the most natural sweet.

Do not eat gravies, or anything thickened with flour.

Do not eat mushes of any kind.

Do not drink tea, coffee, chocolate or cocoa.

Do not eat or drink anything ice cold.

Do not drink anything very hot.

Do not drink any alcoholic liquors.

Do not use tobacco in any form.

Do not use pepsin digestants.

Generally speaking, eat twice as long as you are in the habit of doing, and eat only one-half as much as you think you need.

Food is a poison to anyone with a fever. But acid fruits are often tolerated. Feeding persons with a fever has killed more people than the fever itself.

All unnatural foods harm the system, by gradually unbalancing the functions. Unnatural foods are those that have been deprived of part of their constituents, as white bread, or refined sugar, or vegetables from which juice has been discarded.

There is no 'specific' food that will 'do you good' any more than there is a 'specific' dope that will make you well, after you have become sick by breaking the laws of nature.

Dr. Starr White talks much sense, but he is inclined to be rather too strict. For example, when he advises no condiments it has to be remembered that a little black or red pepper can be a useful digestive stimulant and a harmless one. He is against all alcohol; but St. Paul told Timothy to take a little wine for his stomach's sake. Wine or stout in strict moderation can have beneficial effects.

FACTS ABOUT FOODS

LESSON 2

Dietetic scientists classify food into proteins, carbohydrates, fats and mineral salts, but not enough attention has been paid to the fact that the mineral salts must be in natural combination (vitamins) or the life-promoting and sustaining properties of foods will not exist.

PROTEINS. These are mainly found in nuts, legumes, flesh foods, eggs, milk. They are also found in plants but to a lesser degree. Chemically all proteins tend to differ one from the other. Nature employs proteins to build tissue and promote energy. Cooking tends to render proteins much less effective, reduce their valuable alkaline content and tends to cause stomach fermentation and a putrid condition. This is an argument in favour of uncooked foods, but they do require very thorough mastication. It is useless asking some people to tackle raw foods if they cannot digest them, and a great deal of harm has been done by trying to make people partake of such foods. However, a little raw food very thoroughly masticated will do good. So it is suggested that those who find difficulty in digesting raw food try taking very small quantities at a time and very thoroughly masticating them. Gradually the digestive organs will learn to utilise and assimilate these foods without causing upset.

The simplest forms of protein are made up of oxygen, carbon, hydrogen and nitrogen, and the more complex forms also contain phosphorus and sulphur. To some extent proteins can replace starches, dextrins and sugars as producers of heat and energy. The building of tissue cells and the work of repair depends on a normal supply of protein foods, which starches, fats and sugars cannot entirely replace.

Protein elements are highly complex and are made up of a variety of chemical units called amino-acids. These amino-acids are essential for the promotion of good health and nutrition. Protein introduced directly into the blood acts like a poison, but after the digestive ferments in the stomach and intestines have reduced the proteins into amino-acids the substance is utilised by the system for the work of repair and body building. Amino-acids extracted from various sources and given on their own fail to produce the desired nutritional effects. It seems that such complex items must be administered in combination with other nutritional substances as provided in the natural associations in normal food. In order to obtain all the necessary elements required for proper nutrition variety in food intake is essential. Thus the cellular intelligence can select what it needs. Mono diets and strict dietetic regimens are likely to fall short of body requirements. Note, however, that in some instances a mono diet for a short period can be most helpful and curative; such as an exclusive diet of Slippery Elm Food for a few days in cases of stomach or duodenal ulceration.

Although an ample supply of good protein food is essential it must be kept in mind that the system cannot deal with such foods adequately without the presence of the vital mineral salts.

In some cases additional protein in the form of milk casein may be advisable. The food known as Sanatogen contains this form of protein, and so does Plasmom, although the latter is not heard of these days.

Observation of families who fed on two meals daily consisting of fruit, nuts, vegetables, honey and olive oil confirms the view that it is not so much quantity but quality that matters, for these families were most healthy and kept free from infectious diseases. No doubt these families never overtaxed their digestive organs, and their organs were able to deal effectively with what was eaten without expending unnecessary energy on unwanted food.

The average adult does not require any more than about two ounces of protein daily, so it is wise not to be obsessed with the idea that one must have 'plenty of protein'. Body energy is also obtained from starches, natural sugars and fats; and an ample intake of fresh air also supplies vitality, as we shall discuss later. The rapidly growing body of an infant is thoroughly nourished by its intake of milk containing less than two per cent protein. That is to say about half an ounce of protein each day.

Thoroughly masticated nuts are a good source of protein. Those who find nuts hard to digest should note the effect of more thorough chewing. Nuts masticated to a pulp are usually well digested, even by a weak stomach.

CARBOHYDRATES. There are two groups of these foods, and their essential elements are carbon and hydrogen. Hence the name of carbohydrates. Oxygen is also present. One group consists of the starches, and the other dextrins and sugar. Through the processes of digestion the starches are changed into dextrins and glucose, cane sugar into levulose and milk sugar into galactose. These are then absorbed in the digestive tract via the cell linings in the intestines into the blood and lymph. Unless starches are thoroughly converted they remain not only useless as nutritional elements, but their partially fermented debris gives rise to cellular obstruction and are a reason for the presence of catarrh, or pathological mucous. Here we have one of the main reasons for auto-toxaemia (self-poisoning).

Many people eat far too much starch and also fail to thoroughly masticate such foods. This is one reason why so many are toxic and suffer as a result from acidity, rheumatic trouble, 'nerviness' and a host of disorders due to the system being too acid and laden with morbid matter.

Orthodox dietetic experts claim that the heat and energy latent in carbonaceous foods is the only source of heat and energy in the human organism. This is a great mistake and can lead to overeating. The value of food cannot be measured by calories or by its general effect upon metabolism. In many instances food of very low calorific value is the most essential and beneficial in sustaining life and energy. Also, it must never be forgotten that the intake of oxygen is vital to sustain energy and the life force. Never worry about how many calories different foods contain. A hundred calories for one may not apply to another. Calories mean the quantity of heat generated by burning a certain quantity of material. Dynamite is very high in calories, and nobody eats dynamite.

Many vegetarians in their anxiety to replace flesh foods partake of far too much starch, and wonder why they still suffer from indigestion, acidity, exhaustion and many other conditions. These people do not manage to digest and assimilate as they should, and the semi-digested residue of food eaten turns into a morbid mess that poisons the system. As far as is reasonably possible partake of dry, uncooked foods and masticate them well. Natural foods can be highly medicinal as well as nutritional.

FATS AND OILS. The excessive eating of certain fats and oils places a strain on the liver and can give rise to cholesterol imbalance, leading to high blood pressure and blood clotting. The latter is responsible for the breakdown of the blood vessels, especially of the hair-like capillaries. When this takes place in the brain a stroke follows. There are two classes of fats: the saturated and the unsaturated. The so-called saturated fats are mostly found in animal tissue, and such fats are a cause for the damage mentioned above. The unsaturated fats are of vegetable origin and include sunflower seeds and maize oils. These oils are excellent for use as salad dressings and for cooking.

It is wise to avoid the saturated fats as far as is reasonably possible, especially when thrombosis, arterial disease and strokes tend to run in the family. Sufferers from heart disorders are also better for avoiding these fats as many heart attacks are due to the use of fats of the saturated variety. Those who are flesh eaters should avoid cooked animal fats and partake of lean meats only.

Fats are chemically composed of carbon, hydrogen and oxygen. But while the melting of sugar liberates water the melting of fats does not, but produces oil only. In the digestive process fats produce heat and energy. Some writers argue that there is absolutely no nutritional value in fats. Such reasoning is faulty. Nature provided small quantities of oil and fats in many foods and the animal organism is designed to deal with such. In cold climates there is an instinctive call for more fat; hence the quantity partaken of by the Eskimos. It would seem that over the centuries nature has adapted the digestive system of various peoples to deal with local climatic conditions. If one partakes of foods that are natural and unfaked, the system will deal with them if they are properly masticated, no matter whether the fats and oils present are saturated or unsaturated. But, as stated above, when certain circulatory conditions exist the sufferer should seek to avoid fats that are saturated.

Fats of milk and eggs, be it noted, are rich in the important fat soluble A vitamin. Vitamins will be dealt with later on. It should be noted that some oils have pronounced curative properties, especially the essential oils of some plants. These are employed extensively in medicines.

MINERAL SALTS. These play a vital part in digestion, assimilation and all organic functional activity. Modern chemicalised foods are always deficient in the mineral salts, and cooking also robs foods of their mineral content. Nutritional experts at one time were mainly concerned with proteins, starches, sugars and fats, but now they are taking far more notice of the mineral salt content of foods, a matter which has received the attention of Nature Cure advocates for many years.

The mineral elements may be divided into two groups: The alkaline and the acid. The alkaline elements are potassium, sodium, calcium, magnesium, iron, manganese and aluminium. Acid forming elements are phosphorus, sulphur, silicon, chlorine, fluorine, iodine and arsenic. These salts, both alkaline and acid, are essential to nutrition. In fact without their presence in proper proportions no body function from the process of thinking to those of digestion, assimilation and elimination could take place. In other words the mind and body without the presence of mineral salts are dead.

The minerals enter the system as fully oxidized compounds, and furnish practically no energy or body heat; yet they hold the key to nearly all life manifestation. They are indispensable .in the formation of cells and tissues; also they convey vital electricity and magnetism, constantly recharging the human life dynamo. Additionally, they are the carriers of life promoting oxygen throughout the system.

They are the purifiers of the blood and the eliminators of systemic waste products, and may be said to form the true materia medica, rendering the body invulnerable to disease invasion from germs and viruses. Mineral salts are the foundation stones upon which real healing must be built.

As far back as 1873 attention had been given to the mineral salts — the essential component parts of the human body. A certain German homoeopathic physician, Dr. Schuessler, became profoundly interested in the part played by minerals in health and disease. Schuessler, being a homoeopath, knew of the great healing value of many mineral salts, and that the curative virtue of plants probably depended on their mineral salt content. He believed that the body was a self-healing mechanism and that disease could be healed by providing nature with the elements peculiar to the substance of the body present in normal health. Schuessler maintained that disease is caused primarily by a deficiency, or a molecular imbalance of mineral salts.

A deficiency or disturbance of calcium leads to disorders of nutrition and of the skeleton, sodium lack leads to digestive disorders, acidity, rheumatism and associated disorders. When the potassium intake is not normal we find blood disorders, toxaemia, cancer and nervous disorders. A shortage or disturbance of magnesium can cause cramps, nervous exhaustion and disorders characterised by sharp pains. Iron, being one of the chief oxygen carriers, is essential to ensure that oxygen is carried throughout the system, and a shortage can cause debility, anaemia, respiratory and circulatory disorders. A lack of silica will result in weakness of both brain and body, and even of deformities in the nails and teeth.

When the body has been reduced to ashes the salts mentioned are found therein, and Schuessler based his system of therapy on administering minute quantities of the salts he discovered in the ash in minute homoeopathic form. The doctor discovered twelve salts, and there is no doubt that their proper administration in homoeopathic form has achieved a great deal of good. To administer the same elements in a crude form cannot produce any good results as the body can deal only with minute quantities as provided in the plant kingdom. In fact to administer crude elements can achieve a great deal of harm. Many take crude soda compounds for indigestion. They experience some ease but have to continue to take sodium, for the cause is never touched. The employment of crude iron compounds only serve to upset digestion and can even be a cause of anaemia for which it is frequently prescribed.

The human body can deal only with mineral matter in the fine form in which it is found in nature's own laboratory (plant life). True, the Schuessler salts were originally crude substances, but the prolonged homoeopathic processing of these salts renders them as fine or finer than they are in vegetable life. It has also been found that people obviously suffering from mineral salt deficiency may be taking more than sufficient of these elements in their food. The trouble is that they are not assimilating them. These people with a calcium shortage will eliminate calcium in their excreta. A few doses of highly potentised calcium will tend to rectify the nutritional fault, proving that the homoeopathic (biochemic) salt acts as a catalyst and enables the system to attract and assimilate its like from the food eaten.

In Schuessler's day the scope of analysis was limited. Now we are well aware that all the minerals found in nature are also present in the system, performing an important function. Hence the trace elements of gold, silver, copper, tin, selenium, cadmium, zinc and all the others have their undoubted function to play in the body. The Schuessler system is far too limited, but as has been said the original twelve mineral salts (the basic salts) have accomplished a great deal of good when administered by competent hands. The homoeopaths employ these elements with outstanding results.

The famous dietetic expert, Otto Carque, wrote a large volume on diet and went very deeply into the subject of nutrition and the part played by the mineral salts. He gave detailed tables showing the mineral content of a large number of foods and provided an interesting and instructive study of the subject. However, much of this is beyond the scope of the average person and our task is to get down to basic facts and present them in an elementary form that can be easily understood.

It is interesting to note that plant disease is due in the main to the same causes affecting humans: a mineral deficiency in the soil. It has also been observed that the proper treatment of the soil results in obtaining disease-free and pest-free vegetation. It is about time we ceased fiddling about with test tubes and animal experimentation and got down to facts, employing nature's way of soil treatment by returning to the earth that which has been taken out of it — by composting. Nature will do the rest.

Generally speaking people eat far too many acid forming foods and not sufficient of the alkaline forming variety. Some of the chief alkaline forming foods are: asparagus, artichokes, beans, beets, cabbage, carrots, cauliflower, celery, cucumber, dandelions, greens, garlic, green peas, lettuce, spinach, sprouts, radishes, mushrooms, parsley, tomatoes, vegetable marrow, watercress, milk, soya beans, peaches, pears, pineapple, oranges, lemons, grapes, grapefruit, honey, nuts, potatoes (cooked in their jackets), egg yolk, apples, onions, straw-berries.

Note that those who find cucumber and radishes hard to digest will find them more acceptable to the stomach if the skin of the cucumber and the tops of radishes are eaten. However, some just cannot tolerate such items of diet until their digestive organs are more healthy.

Acid forming foods should be taken in strict moderation, for most people are far too acid. Acid forming foods are: all starches, polished rice, refined breakfast cereals, white flour, pastry, cakes, most puddings, all flesh foods, fish and fowl, fats and oils (except butter), jams, sweets, preserves, alcohol, white sugar, tea, coffee, cocoa, chocolate, synthetic soft drinks.

The ratio of about four alkaline to one acid food is a good guide. But never worry about being exact. Worry of any kind, even over food itself, depletes and causes indigestion. The most miserable and unhealthy people the writer has met are those who fuss too much over diet. These people are very introspective and dwell too much on themselves. Just use common sense and be happy and of good cheer.

POTASSIUM. This is found in all brain and body cells. Cell construction and renewal would be impossible without the presence of this salt, and especially of the cells of the brain and nervous system. It helps nature to throw off pathological material and is of great value in nervous and general debility. softening of the brain, heart disorders (especially of nervous origin), neuralgias, hysteria, headaches, insomnia, muscular atrophy, blood poisoning, a tendency to malignancy, sluggish digestion, asthma, sore throats, bronchitis, catarrh, influenza, measles and skin disorders, skin inactivity, anaemia and dandruff.

Foods rich in potassium are: apples (very rich), apricots (very rich), blackberries (very rich), cherries (rich), cranberries (rich), currants — especially black (very rich), gooseberries (rich), grapes (rich), huckleberries (very rich), peaches (rich), plums (rich), prunes (rich), raspberries (rich), straw-berries (rich), watermelons (rich), bananas, dates (rich), figs,

29

olives, oranges, grapefruit, lemons (rich), limes, pineapple (rich), pomegranate, prunes, raisins, nuts, artichokes, asparagus, beets, sprouts, cabbage (especially red), carrots, cauliflower, celery, chicory, chives, cucumbers, dandelions (very rich), dill, eggplant, horseradish, kale (very rich), leeks, lettuce (very rich), onions, green peppers, potatoes (with jackets), radishes, rhubarb (very rich), sorrel (very rich), spinach, tomatoes (very rich), turnips (very rich), watercress (very rich), whole barley, buckwheat, corn-on-the-cob, millet oats, whole rice, rye, wheat, wholemeal bread, rye bread, caraway seed, sunflower seed, mushrooms, truffles, milk, flesh foods.

SODIUM. This promotes nutrition and is contained in every fluid and solid of the body; without this salt the body would be starved. It does much to keep the system alkaline and has the power to change substances into different compounds without changing itself. It is useful in all acid, urine and rheumatic conditions and does much to prevent jaundice and gall stones. Sodium is of value in catarrh, diarrhoea, indigestion, dropsy, scurvy, malaria, sunstroke, insect stings, teething troubles, flatulence, skin disorders, malignancy, asthma, disorders of the prostate gland, etc.

Foods rich in sodium are: apples, apricots, gooseberries, pears, prunes (very rich), raspberries, strawberries (very rich), watermelons, bananas (very rich), figs (very rich), olives, pineapple, pomegranate (very rich), raisins (rich), currants (rich), beechnuts, coconuts, peanuts, artichokes, asparagus (very rich), beets (rich), sprouts, cabbage (very rich), carrots (very rich), celery (exceptionally rich – hence its value in acid states and rheumatism), chicory, chives, cucumbers, dandelions (very rich), garlic, horseradish, kale, leeks (rich), lettuce (rich), onions, radishes, pumpkins (rich), potatoes, rhubarb, salsify, swiss chard (very rich), tomatoes (very rich), turnips, watercress, barley, corn-on-the-cob, millet, oats, whole rice, whole wheat (rich), rye, caraway seed (rich), mustard seed, sunflower seed, mushrooms, truffles, kidney

30

beans, lima beans (rich), raw sugar, buttermilk, milk (rich), cheese, eggs, flesh foods.

CALCIUM. This is the master-builder of the body, especially of the bones, teeth, elastic fibres and blood vessels. It promotes the normal activity of the liver and gall bladder and has a 'sweetening' effect on the entire organism. Calcium has a pronounced tonic action and is of value in all prolapsed conditions, varicose veins, ulcers, heart weakness, spinal curvature, anaemia, lung weakness, weakening discharges, catarrh, skin disorders, emaciation, teething trouble, hydrocele, pancreatic weakness, gumboils, boils, enlarged glands, diseases of the connective tissues and faulty metabolism. There is scarcely a disorder in which this salt is not of value.

Foods rich in calcium are: apples, apricots, blackberries (rich), cherries, cranberries (rich), currants, gooseberries, grapes, huckleberries, pears, peaches (rich), plums, prunes (rich), raspberries, strawberries (rich), watermelons, bananas, dates, figs (rich), grapefruit, lemons (rich), limes (rich), olives, oranges (rich), pineapple (rich), pomegranate, prunes, raisins (rich), currants, nuts (rich), artichokes, asparagus (rich), beets (rich), sprouts, cabbage, especially red (very rich), carrots (very rich), cauliflower, celery (exceptionally rich), chicory, chives, cucumbers, dandelions (exceptionally rich), dill (exceptionally rich), horseradish (rich), kale (very rich), leeks (rich), lettuce (very rich), onions (rich), parsley (rich), parsnips, potatoes, pumpkins, radishes, rhubarb (rich), salsify, sorrel, spinach (very rich), tomatoes (rich), turnips (rich), watercress (very rich), whole barley, buckwheat, oats (rich), whole rice, whole rye, wheat bran, wholemeal bread, caraway seeds (rich), mustard seeds, sunflower seeds, truffles, milk, fresh foods.

MAGNESIUM. This is found in the brain, blood cells, spinal cord, muscles, teeth and bones. It seems to work with potassium and is of great value in nervous and spasmodic conditions. This salt is remedial in most cases of cramps, trembling, twitching and pains that are sharp and piercing in nature. Hence its curative effect in neuralgia and neuritis, toothache that is better for the application of warmth, colic, nervous indigestion, prostate gland troubles and exhaustion. Mental and nervous tension call for both potassium and magnesium.

Foods rich in magnesium are: apples (rich), apricots, blackberries (very rich), cherries, gooseberries, huckleberries (rich), grapes, mulberries, peaches, plums (rich), prunes, raspberries, watermelons, bananas (rich), dates, figs (rich), grapefruit, lemons, limes, pineapple (rich), raisins (rich), currants, beechnuts, almonds, brazil nuts and nuts in general, most being rich in magnesium, peanuts, artichokes, asparagus (rich), beets (rich), sprouts (rich), cabbage (very rich), carrots, cauliflower (rich), celery (very rich), chicory, chives, cucumbers, dandelions (very rich), dill (very rich), horseradish, kale (very rich), leeks (rich), lettuce (very rich), onions (rich), parsley (rich), parsnips (rich), potatoes, radishes, salsify, sorrel (rich), spinach (very rich), swiss chard (very rich), tomatoes (very rich), turnips, watercress (very rich), whole barley (rich), whole rye, buckwheat (rich), corn-on-the-cob, millet (rich), whole rice (rich), whole wheat (rich), caraway seed (rich), mustard seed (rich), sunflower seed, mushrooms, truffles (very rich), beans, peas, kidney beans (very rich), soya beans (rich), molasses, milk, goat's milk (rich), cream, cheese, white of eggs, flesh foods, fish.

IRON. This is the chief oxygen carrier, so the value of deep, rhythmic breathing depends to a large extent on the presence of highly organised iron in the system to carry the oxygen to where it is needed. More about breathing will be discussed later on. Iron is found mainly in the blood. A deficiency of iron results in toxic states, anaemia, malnutrition and degeneration of the blood vessels. In all states of fever and inflammation the system calls for more oxygen to 'burn up' the causative waste products, so iron is necessary in neurasthenia, all disorders ending with itis (inflammation) (eyeritis, nephritis, tonsillitis, carditis etc.), inflammatory rheumatism, haemo rrhages, bleeding piles, injuries and usually for pains made better by cold applications (the opposite of magnesium).

Note that iron is not the only salt necessary in anaemia, for calcium, sodium and potassium are equally important. The iron the system can utilise must be that found in plant life, or as prepared by the homoeopaths and biochemists.

Foods rich in iron are: all fresh and dried fruits in small quantities, strawberries (rich), watermelons, traces are found in most nuts, artichokes, asparagus, beets, cabbage, especially red, celery, cucumbers, dandelions, horseradish, kale, leeks (rich), lettuce (very rich), onions, radishes, rhubarb (rich), salsify, sorrel, spinach (very rich), tomatoes, turnips. Traces are found in all whole grain, more especially in whole rice and rye, wholemeal bread, caraway seed (rich), mushrooms, truffles, liver, bone meal (very rich). Flesh foods have traces. Milk.

PHOSPHORUS. This is regarded as the supreme brain food, although the homoeopaths and biochemists usually give it in combination with potassium (kali phos.). Phosphorus promotes brain and bone metabolism, increases the number of red blood corpuscles and improves nutrition. Many homoeopaths advise phosphorus in one form or another as essential to the recovery of nervous disorders, and also in some respiratory infections. Several of the advertised nerve foods contain phosphorus.

Phosphorus rich foods are: apples (very rich), apricots (rich), blackberries (very rich), cherries (rich), cranberries, currants, especially red and black, gooseberries (very rich), grapes (rich), huckleberries (very rich), nectarines, pears (rich), peaches (very rich), plums (rich), prunes (very rich), raspberries (rich), strawberries (very rich), watermelons (very rich), bananas (rich), dates, figs (very rich), grapefruit, lemons (very rich), limes (very rich), mango, pomegranate, raisins (very rich), almonds (very rich), beechnuts (very rich), brazil nuts (very rich), chestnuts (very rich), coconuts, walnuts, (very rich), peanuts (very rich), artichokes (very rich), asparagus (very rich), beets (very rich), sprouts (exceptionally rich), cabbage (rich), cauliflower (rich), celery (very rich), chives, cucumbers (very rich), dandelions (very rich), dill (rich), horseradish, kale (exceptionally rich), leeks (very rich), lettuce (very rich), onions (rich), parsley (rich), potatoes (rich), pumpkins (very rich), radishes (exceptionally rich), rhubarb (rich), salsify, sorrel (very rich), swiss chard, tomatoes (very rich), turnips (very rich), watercress (very rich), whole barley (rich), buckwheat (rich), corn-on-the-cob, oats (rich), whole rice (rich), whole rye (rich), whole wheat (rich) (wheat germ is exceptionally rich), wholemeal bread (rich), caraway seed (very rich), mustard seed (very rich), sunflower seed (very rich), mushrooms (exceptionally rich), truffles (exceptionally rich), milk (rich), eggs, flesh foods contain traces, bone meal is exceptionally rich, beef and chicken (rich), fish (very rich). It will be noted that foods considered to be of little value by many orthodox dietetic experts are rich in minerals, such as mushrooms and the fruit and vegetable families. Always these people are concerned with proteins, starches, sugars, fats and the almighty calorie!

SULPHUR. This is the chief blood and systemic cleanser. The homoeopaths give it in its potentised form, or in combination such as kali sulph., natrum sulph., etc. They have a saying: 'When in doubt give sulphur', which means that they know that the basic cause for so many complaints is a morbid state of the system, and if the cleansing sulphur is administered good is bound to result.

Sulphur is indicated for all toxic states and is positively anti-psoric. That is to say that it deals with the toxic causes of a host of ailments due to a toxic state, impure blood and lymph. It works wonders in cases where there are offensive discharges, skin diseases, burning, itching and general inertia.

Foods containing sulphur are: apples, artichokes, blackberries, cherries, cranberries (very rich), currants, gooseberries, grapes, pears, peaches (rich), plums, prunes, raspberries (very rich), strawberries (rich), watermelons (rich), bananas, dates, figs (rich), grapefruit, lemons, limes (rich), olives, pineapple (rich), raisins (rich), beechnuts, brazil nuts (rich), chestnuts,

34

filberts, traces in all other nuts, artichokes, asparagus (rich), beets (very rich), sprouts (exceptionally rich), cabbage (rich), carrots (very rich), cauliflower (rich), celery (rich), chives (rich), cucumbers (rich), dandelions, dill (very rich), horseradish (very rich), kale (exceptionally rich), leeks (rich), lettuce (rich), onions (rich), parsnips (rich), potatoes, radishes (rich), rhubarb, salsify (rich), sorrel (very rich), spinach (very rich), swiss chard (rich), tomatoes (rich), turnips (very rich), watercress (exceptionally rich), all whole grain (average to rich) (especially whole wheat, rye and oats). wholemeal bread, caraway seed, mustard seed, mushrooms, truffles, beans, lentils, peas, cocoa, chocolate, milk, cheese, eggs, fish in general (rich), beef, chicken.

SILICON (SILICA). This serves as a strengthening agent and is found in the brain, nerves, connective tissues, teeth and bones. A deficiency can cause a lack of mental concentration, anxiety, local swellings, nervous disorders etc. Homoeopathic doses enable the system to throw off accumulated pus, hence it is indicated in boils and swellings, hardened glands etc. It has been termed the lancet of homoeopathy. Of value in disorders affecting the teeth and hair.

Foods containing silicon (silica) are: apples, apricots, cherries, prunes, strawberries (rich), watermelons, figs, beechnuts, lettuce (very rich), asparagus (rich), beets (rich), sprouts, cauliflower, cabbage, celery, cucumber (rich), dandelions, (rich), dill, horseradish (rich), leeks, parsley (rich), pumpkins, radishes (rich), rhubarb, swiss chard, tomatoes, turnips, millet, whole rice (rich). (All wholegrains contain traces), caraway seed, mustard seed, sunflower seed (rich), peas. (Traces are found in all dairy products).

Bamboo shoots are exceptionally rich in silica.

Although exact analysis has not been made of many wild herbs it can be stated that herbs growing in the wild are all very rich in all the vital mineral salts, trace elements and vitamins, which is a reason for the success in healing of herbal therapy.

CHLORINE. This does much to regulate the body fluids. It aids the functions of digestion and elimination, and is of special value in catarrhal conditions, fevers and respiratory troubles. Homoeopathically it is mostly given in the form of kali mur. (potassium chloride) and natrum mur. (sodium chloride).

Chlorine foods: blackberries, (traces are found in all fresh fruits), raspberries, strawberries, watermelons, rose hips, figs, limes olives, pineapple, raisins, currants, beechnuts, artichokes, asparagus, beets (rich), sprouts, cabbage (rich), red cabbage (very rich), carrots (rich), cauliflower, celery, chicory (very rich), chives, cucumbers (rich), dandelions, dill (very rich), leeks, lettuce (exceptionally rich), onions, potatoes, radishes, spinach, swiss chard (rich), tomatoes (exceptionally rich), turnips (rich), watercress (rich), corn-on-the-cob, oats (traces are found in all whole grain), wholemeal bread, caraway seed, truffles, beans, lentils, cocoa beans, milk (rich), goat's milk (very rich), cheese (very rich), eggs (yolks very rich), fish (rich).

The trace elements such as gold, silver, copper, antimony, iodine, cadmium, erbium, iodine, thorium, titanium, iridium, arsenic, mercury, lead, neodyum, platinum, radium, selenium, samarium, strontia, tin, tantalum, zinc etc., are found in minute traces in many natural foods, but detailed analysis is lacking. The wild herbs are the richest sources. Iodine, for example, is found to be present in seaweed (kelp). Kelp will be discussed later.

One cannot always regard tables of mineral content in various foods to be absolutely accurate, especially with respect to vegetation, as the locality, nature of the soil and even the season of the year when gathered will make a difference in the results of analysis.

In this presentation of dietetics it is unnecessary to give percentage tables, and to do so would only serve to confuse the reader. The object is to present the subject as simply as possible and to deal with fundamentals and essentials. What it all boils down to is the fact that when one partakes of a variety of natural, properly grown foods one will obtain all the minerals necessary to attain and maintain good health,

36

always provided that the foods eaten are well masticated.

Some writers claim that the mineral salts are the carriers of vitamins. We do know that organised minerals are essential to vitamin formation, and that without minerals there would not be any vitamins. The nature of any substance depends on the number and arrangement of its atoms and molecules. Likewise, the number and arrangement of the mineral salts determine the nature of vitamins.

BREAD

LESSON 3

'Give us this day our daily bread'. Bread could of course refer to food in a general sense, but bread made from grain seems to be the obvious item. A human being could exist on bread alone if it were made from whole grain. The pasty rubbish sold in the shops is a poor apology for the real thing. Wholemeal bread is 'a staff of life', but the white variety is the road to death.

Whole wheat contains the elements necessary to sustain life; bread made from white, refined flour falls far below the body's requirements. In 1,000 parts of water-free substance genuine whole wheat bread yields a total of about 23.30 parts of mineral matter, while white bread yields about 17 parts.

Rats of the same family were divided into two groups. One was fed entirely on wholemeal bread and the other on white bread. The former grew vigorously, and were fat and well with glossy coats. The latter soon became skinny, weak, lethargic and puny with dull coats, and died. The writer has observed this experiment himself, and it proves beyond all question the vast superiority of wholemeal bread.

38

The processing to rob the flour of its mineral content is without sense, for to make good the calcium loss the baker has by law to replace the calcium with crude lime. Visit any flour mill and you will find a pile of lime which is shovelled into the flour for dough making.

Many say they can eat plenty of white bread, but find they do not want much wholemeal. The reason is that the body calls for nourishment which the white bread cannot supply, so they crave to get that 'full up' feeling, and that means that the stomach is over-packed with food that does not really nourish, but tends to form a gas and cause indigestion and constipation. Wholemeal bread tastes nutty and satisfies, especially when it is well masticated.

Brown bread as sold in the shops is not genuine wholemeal. Always insist on bread made from the whole wheat. More and more people are baking their own bread with wholemeal flour, such as Allinson's and Prewett's. Such wholemeal bread is delicious and very satisfying. Also, to make bread at home is cheaper than purchasing from the shops, and one knows what one is eating. Bread at home can be made with or without yeast.

It is interesting to note that an acre of land devoted to wheat may produce nearly ten times as much protein as the same acre devoted to pasturage for beef cattle. The same quantity of land devoted to nut cultivation will produce a still larger amount of good protein. Thus, from an economic standpoint the raising of crops has an advantage over the production of animals for food purposes.

To return to bread and the problem of yeast: many who oppose the employment of yeast say that fermented bread contains alcohol. In reply, it is known that yeast germs die at a high temperature and cannot survive the heat of the baking oven. Opponents of yeast maintain that the 'raising' of dough is due to gases arising from the decaying bodies of dead yeast germs. But physiology teaches us that the various processes of digestion are actually completed in the intestines by germ fermentation. The processes of digestion which are left un-done by the enzymes are completed in the intestinal canal by

39

bacterial fermentation. All the processes of digestion from beginning to end are in a sense processes of fermentation. So what difference does it make if a few yeast germs enter the body with the bread eaten?

There is ample proof that the intake of yeast adds to physical energy and has decided tonic value. So the house-wife is at liberty to make her wholemeal bread with or without yeast. Methods for home baking abound in many books, and the simpler the process the better.

The objection to fermented bread in that it tends to create alcohol calls for qualification. The very small quantity of alcohol produced actually plays an important part in the system, adding to functional activity. On the other hand taken to excess alcohol tends to paralyze the inhibitory nervous system, causing temporary overstimulation and resultant exhaustion, and even loss of consciousness.

Yeast is rich in vitamin B and does a great deal to improve the brain and nervous system. The addition of yeast to dough aids to some extent the predigestion of bread and helps to liberate food energy.

VEGETARIANISM. This course is intended for both flesh eaters and vegetarians. As to whether vegetarianism is superior to meat eating is a question that calls for much consideration. It seems obvious that the human family is designed to deal with fruits, nuts, grains and cereals, but it must keep in mind that for many centuries people have been accustomed to meat eating. The fact has to be faced that a few cannot get along without animal food in some form or other; others can manage very well. Apart from the ethical objection to destroy-ing life in order to live there are sound arguments in favour of vegetarianism. For example: the intestine of the animal which exists on flesh is shorter than that of the vegetarian animal. Nature has provided the former with a shorter bowel so that food residue is eliminated more quickly. Flesh foods set up bowel toxaemia much more quickly than is the case with vegetable produce. On the other hand the intestine of the human being is longer so that it can deal with roughage and other vegetable substances. Vegetable food, when properly masticated, does not set up nearly as much putrifaction as is the case with flesh foods. We are reminded of the old Biblical statement: 'The fruit of the tree shall be for food, and the leaf thereof for medicine.' (Ezekiel 47:12). The writer of Genesis also infers that man in his early days fed off the produce of the earth. (Genesis 1:29).

The teeth of a human being are also more adapted to a vegetarian diet, although they can deal effectively with flesh foods. There is ample evidence to prove that the human digestive system deals more effectively with vegetable foods, although once again it must be stressed that thorough mastication is called for. Fruits, nuts, cereals, grain, beans and all vegetables supply real nourishment in a better form than is supplied by flesh foods. Yet it must be kept in mind that the average human is used to flesh foods and has managed very well on them. To change suddenly from a flesh to a totally vegetarian diet is asking for trouble. The ideal on paper does not apply in all cases, and a few people seem to demand the animal force or magnetism supplied by the animal creation.

Most people are so accustomed to soft, mushy foods that they have almost forgotten how to chew. Masticate and enjoy your food and it will nourish and fortify you. Take time over meals. We wonder why everybody is in such a hurry? Haste is upsetting to mind and body — cultivate the habit of being still and thus recharge the system with vital force.

There are some vegetarians who exclude dairy products and eggs from their daily food. They overlook the fact that there is something in animal food that they cannot derive from vegetation, and that is the animal life principle or magnetism. However, when the body is properly nourished it is true to say that animal magnetism is generated within the body. For those who are very lacking in natural magnetism the addition to the diet of dairy products seems to be essential.

The forces or energies at work in the vegetable kingdom are not the highest expression of life force, and there is a higher quality of energy in animal food. The vegetation absorbs

41

sun energy, and in flesh food we also have this sun energy, and in a rather more advanced form. But the truly healthy individual will create his own energy from vegetable food plus the intake of oxygen via the function of breathing.

We have known very sick vegetarians who would not touch dairy produce, and if such people would partake of a little of the animal products they would soon experience better health. We are mainly concerned with those who are not truly fit and well, and although we favour vegetarianism there is ample evidence that a certain quantity of animal food in some form seems to be essential for health and body building. Ideas and ideals are all very well, and are to be aimed for, but in the treatment of the unwell facts have to be faced. No doubt the time will come when nothing shall hurt or destroy — that time is not yet.

It is not easy and certainly not wise to put before the reader a set of rules for daily feeding which will suit everybody. The following has to be regarded as a general guide only to sensible feeding in order to attain and maintain reasonably good health.

1 For those who partake of flesh foods it is wise to keep to beef, mutton, white fish (not fried if you have any digestive trouble) and poultry. Where there is a tendency to blood clotting or high blood pressure avoid cooked animal fats and have lean only. Shell fish, game and the the flesh of the pig are not health-promoting. The rules in the book of Leviticus pertaining to permissible foods is sound sense, and borne out by scientific investigation.

2 As far as is reasonably possible avoid or strictly limit 'fancy', sugary foods, very sweet cakes and pastry. Be moderate with plain cake and when possible have cake made with wholemeal or part wholemeal flour.

3 Bread should be genuine wholemeal. Bread without roughage (such as Hovis) may be eaten by those with very weak digestion, although roughage (bran) is good for constipation and activates the colon. Fresh bread, even wholemeal, is hard to digest and is better eaten

stale, especially when the stomach is weak. Crisp rye bread (or biscuits) suits some weakly folk more than does wheaten bread.

4   Endeavour to have one good fresh salad daily, which should be well masticated. A salad may consist of shredded cabbage, watercress, lettuce, grated sprouts or greens, comfrey leaves, nasturtium leaves or seeds, clover flowers, dandelion leaves, raw or cooked beets, etc. Permitted meats may be taken with salads, or cheese — cottage cheese suits many who cannot tolerate the ordinary Cheddar type. The latter is much more easily digested if cut into thin wafers or grated and spread out on a dish to dry for at least twenty-four hours before eating. Nuts may replace meat with salads, but do not have nuts, meat or cheese at the same meal. Seek to take only one type of protein food at a time.

5   Fresh eggs, lightly boiled or scrambled, in moderation are excellent for most people. May be taken with salads or starchy foods, but should not be combined with flesh foods or cheese.

6   Fresh fruits as available. Sliced or grated apples go well with salads; so also do dates, raisins, figs or sultanas.

7   Late suppers are not advisable for most people, especially those with weak digestions, or who sleep poorly. On the other hand a cup of dandelion coffee, malted milk, slippery elm food or peppermint tea may help to promote refreshing sleep. Yeast beverages or 'Vecon' are also permissible. These are excellent as sandwich spreads during the day.

8   Those who suffer from acidity, rheumatism or sluggish bowels will find quarter to half a teaspoonful of raw molasses dissolved in hot water very remedial. May be taken at any time when thirsty, but especially in the morning. Has some value in anaemia. Sufferers from constipation should dissolve a little molasses in a cup of hot water with four or five prunes added. The prunes will absorb most or all of the molasses water over night.

Take for breakfast with a helping of wheat germ and any good bran cereal.

9   A little wheat germ ('Froment', Bemax' etc.) may be sprinkled over any food at any time. Beneficial to brain, nerves and the system in general.

10 Tea should be on the weak side. China or Maté tea are more healthful than Indian or Ceylon. Dandelion coffee or Instant Postum will replace ordinary coffee. The latter tends to disturb sleep. On the other hand a cup of ordinary black coffee after a meal will aid digestion. In spite of all that has been written against it, black coffee taken in strict moderation has a pronounced tonic value. This has been confirmed by the celebrated and broad-minded Dr. Bernard Aschner. Diluted fruit or vegetable juices, tomato juice, etc., are excellent beverages. Fresh milk may suit some but not all people. The younger you are the more your system is likely to take to milk; but have milk on its own and sip it slowly. Soft water is curative, but that supplied by the average tap is highly suspect and chemically contaminated. Boil water before taking internally if at all uncertain. A glass of beer or stout taken on occasions will not hurt anybody and both have food and tonic value. We are not concerned with fads but with proven facts. Use your intelligence and note the effects of foods and beverages on your system. Shun what does not agree with you. Spirits are not recommended except for medicinal reasons. What you eat or drink may not please or suit your neighbour. It is noteworthy that St. Paul told Timothy to 'take a little wine for his stomach's sake'. It is the abuse of these things that is so bad. One can have too much even of the very good. Be moderate in all things.

11 Eat or drink only when hungry or thirsty, not just because it is meal time. When hungry you will enjoy your food. In spite of what the writer or anybody else has to say do not eat or drink what does not appeal to the palate, for the stomach tends to reject such items.

12 Simplicity and thorough mastication are the keynotes of

44

sane diet. Never eat when mentally upset or angry. Be happy at the meal table.

13 Avoid the heavy use of condiments and vinegar use lemon juice instead. But a little black or red pepper is good for the digestion. The less table salt the better, and what you use should be sea salt for preference. With pure, natural foods you do not have the need for condiments.

14 Shun white sugar and sugary foods. They cause acidity and ruin the teeth. Moist brown sugar in moderation is in order, but pure honey is the best sweetener. Honey will be discussed later on.

15 Do not cook in aluminium pots or pans as they poison both food and beverages. Use stainless steel, iron, tin, glass or good enamel.

16 Real soda water (which actually does not contain soda) may be taken after meals if there is any indigestion.

17 When on a special diet (as for diabetes) keep to what the practitioner has advised.

18 Vegetables etc. should be either steamed or cooked conservatively to conserve the valuable minerals and vitamins.

19 Do not be afraid of food, for the fear is even worse than the dietetic errors.

20 Visit the dentist regularly. Decayed teeth interfere with proper mastication and a septic root can be a focal point of infection, causing a toxic condition.

21 When at all possible take a rest — even if only a brief one — after any heavy meal. This is done by the animals.

SUGGESTIONS FOR DAILY MEALS

BREAKFAST

1 Stale wholemeal bread or toast with a moderate quantity of butter, vegetable margarine or nut butter. Rye or wholemeal biscuits.

or

2   Any popular breakfast cereal with wheat germ ('Bemax' or 'Froment') added. Constipated people should add soaked prunes with about a quarter of a teaspoonful of molasses. Prunes may be soaked in a cup of hot water overnight, to which the molasses can be added. For a change black figs, sultanas or raisins may be taken.

or

3   Oat porridge, or porridge made from coarse wholemeal flour.

or

4   A lightly boiled or scrambled fresh egg on toast, providing eggs agree.

Note: Yeast extract or 'Vecon' may be used on bread or toast at any time.

LUNCH

1   A fresh salad is advisable. This may consist of any green, leafy vegetables in season: cabbage, watercress, lettuce, nasturtium seeds, clover flowers, dandelion leaves, comfrey leaves, etc., etc. Add dried Cheddar or cottage cheese, or use grated nuts in place of cheese; or have flesh food instead of cheese or nuts, but never have more than one kind of protein food at the same meal. Stale wholemeal bread with a little butter, or potatoes baked or boiled in their jackets, but not both bread and potatoes. The salad may be dressed with olive, sunflower seed oil or corn oil, plus a little fresh lemon juice instead of vinegar. Follow with a natural sweet if desired. Do not use white sugar; but pure honey or moist brown sugar is permissible.

or

2   Permitted meats, poultry or steamed white fish with conservatively cooked vegetables (Potatoes to be baked or boiled in their skins). Those with good digestions can eat the jackets of cooked potatoes. Vegetarians may have nuts, cheese or beans in place of meat.

or

46

3   Vegetable stew or thick soup followed by a natural sweet or bread pudding. Wholemeal rice pudding is in order.

1   Apart from a beverage tea is usually an unnecessary meal. Never eat unless really hungry. If desired have one of the meals suggested for breakfast.
2   Baked beans or a scrambled egg on wholemeal toast (if hungry).
3   A small salad with wholemeal bread and butter, or wholemeal biscuits. Plain cake if desired.

Most people are better without supper. A late meal tends to keep some people restless at night, while others find a small meal will promote sleep. All may benefit from a cup of 'Vecon', slippery elm food, 'Benger's Food', 'Complan' or dandelion coffee. Others may have a small glass of stout or beer, or malted milk. Keep to what seems to suit you best.

Should you feel the need of condiments with cooked food or salads keep to red or black pepper, and sea salt in moderation. As already suggested fresh lemon juice should replace vinegar.

One fairly heavy meal daily is sufficient. Others should be on the light side. Above all eat only when really hungry and well masticate. Never worry over food or digestion will suffer. Pickles are not recommended, but for the average healthy person just a little may be eaten on occasions.

No matter what has been said respecting meals it must be kept in mind that just a few people manage better by having several very small meals during the day instead of eating heavy meals at fixed times; but no snacks between meals. It is for each individual to find out what suits him or her best. Be sure to have mineral-rich foods whatever system you adopt. If in doubt about taking a sufficient supply of mineral matter it is suggested that one or two plain kelp (seaweed) tablets be chewed with every meal.

The writer spent a year in a famous British Nature Cure establishment where the chief cure for all manner of diseases was fasting. In this respect the health home was similar to several of the European health homes where fasting, water treatment, massage, dieting and (sometimes) herbal medicines are the methods employed. The names of some of the great nature cure pioneers comes to mind, such as Biltz, Lindlahr, Kneipp and Schrot. The two former embraced nature cure in general and were prolific writers on the natural treatment of illness, while Kneipp concentrated mainly on water treatments (hydrotherapy) and herbalism. Schrot perfected his special system of liquid-restrictive diet.

There is no doubt whatever that going without food is nature's main method of eliminating the causes of disease and the method adopted instinctively by the animal creation when they are ill. No form of persuasion can tempt an animal to eat when it is unwell. Of this deeply seated habit we should pay special note.

Under expert supervision the writer has observed even the most serious disorders responding to short or long fasts, the duration of which depended largely on the nature of the disorders and the vitality of the sufferer. Even malignancy has yielded to this method.

Blinded by pseudo-science, orthodox practitioners seem to do all they can to get the sick to eat when they are ill, 'to keep up their strength', when the unfortunate sufferer instinctively rebels against all food. They forget that the sick organism is not capable of dealing with food at such times, and that food in such circumstances even places an added strain on the vitality of the sufferer. Of course fear plays a part, and as has been said before fear is a real disease itself.

As we shall see, only a part of our energy comes from food; a major part comes from oxygen intake. People tend to believe all they are told by those who think they know all the answers, and if they are informed that they must eat when they are ill they make an effort to partake of what instinct and appetite resists. Practically everybody would be better in health if they had a short fast of one to three days every few weeks, thus cleansing the system of toxic substances (the basic cause for disease) and balancing up the constitution.

Prolonged fasts should be undertaken only under expert supervision, but a short fast can be undertaken by most people without any possibility of harm resulting. Under a fast the total resources of the organism are devoted to the essential work of cleansing, healing and restoration. On a fast body poisons are rapidly eliminated from the blood and tissues, and passed off through the usual channels: lungs, skin, kidneys and bowels.

On a fast the breath becomes foul, the tongue coated and the body aroma unpleasant. There may be headaches – due to the liberation of toxic substances and the faster may become low in spirits. As a rule after about three days all unpleasant symptoms disappear. The possible hungry feeling passes off and the faster becomes more 'alive'. True hunger is eventually evidenced by a watering of the mouth, showing that the saliva is being secreted for the first essential process of digestion. Unpleasant symptoms vary in different people, and in some cases may scarcely manifest. It may be added that to go without food for a single day, or even one meal, will often accomplish all that is necessary to rectify many stomach and digestive upsets.

During a fast take plenty of water; distilled water being the best, although this is not essential. Flavour with fresh fruit juice if desired, and take slowly, in sips. In winter be sure to keep warm. The first meal following a short fast should consist of fresh fruit or a small salad, and again it is stressed that mastication should be thorough. If necessary during a fast keep the bowels open, even if you have to employ a mild purgative; but leave off any purgative when bowel movement has been achieved.

In cases of stomach or duodenal ulceration or inflammation (gastritis), it is sometimes advisable to take a cup of any good slippery elm food once to three times daily. This will pro-

49

mote healing; but as a rule it is better to avoid all food of any nature. Naturally, one has to use will power to go on a fast. That is what the will is for. Fasting (even a very short one) helps to keep the body in subjection, hence the reason why it is a spiritual exercise advocated by all the great spiritual teachers. Anything demanding the employment of the will helps to build character. God does not tend to make use of an unclean tabernacle, so we have to strive to be clean within.

Regarding the use of purgatives: many will find an enema quite effective, and we find this to be more logical than taking medicine.

VITAMINS

LESSON 4

Great emphasis is laid on the importance of vitamins in these days. Yet, not so long ago, they had never been heard of! One sometimes wonders how the human family managed to survive for thousands of years without knowing anything about these vital food elements. The truth is that all truly natural foods are vitamin-rich, but since they have been 'discovered' and isolated, a unique opportunity has taken place for the greedy to make capital out of supplying these substances without which we cannot exist. Of course vitamins cannot be over-rated, yet they can be taken to excess and many spend a great deal of money purchasing these elusive substances in tablet form when they could obtain their vitamin requirements from natural foods. As with the mineral salts (with which vitamins are closely related) commercialism has robbed natural foods of their vitamin content and made money by replacing them with man-made products, some of which are synthetic in nature and not nearly so good as the vitamins supplied by nature in their natural setting. Indeed, it is possible to suffer from vitamin poisoning. Too much of a good thing can be a disadvantage and even dangerous. How-

51

ever, some vitamins cannot be taken to excess, such as vitamin C, which the system can utilise in fair quantities daily.

Dr. George Starr White says that vitamins are the natural salts in natural combination. He adds that the process of cooking changes the natural combinations of the salts, and therefore destroys the vitamins. It has been proved that this is the case; so cooking, especially for lengthy periods, robs the food of many of its essential qualities. Some cooks not only over-cook vegetables, but greens are squeezed between plates to press out the valuable juices, and what is eaten is little better than rubbish. All vegetables should be eaten raw, cooked very conservatively or steamed.

The scientific discovery of vitamins goes back to 1912. Like the enzymes they appear to be mainly composed of carbon, hydrogen, oxygen and nitrogen, but their arrangement is different. They must be chemically united with organic compounds and minerals as found in natural foods, and they are very closely connected with the salts in plant and vegetable life.

The word vitamin is derived from the Latin words vita and amins, or amino acids, which are the component parts of protoplasm. These two words mean 'life'. So vitamins are life-promoting substances. Several of these vitamins have been discovered, A, B and C were the first to receive attention; others followed and each is given a letter of the alphabet. No doubt food scientists will eventually find vitamins all the way from A to Z, and humanity will not be one whit better for the discoveries, for all the vitamins are present in pure, natural food. This cannot be stressed too much.

VITAMIN A. This vitamin is found in milk, cream, butter, cheese, palm oil, fish oils (such as cod and halibut) etc. It is termed fat soluble A. It is also present in cabbage, spinach, lettuce, carrots, corn, tomatoes, potatoes and peas. The dairy products are the richest source. It is, however, claimed that the solids of spinach and tomatoes contain more of A than does butter fat. Vitamin A is a great growth promoter, and is of special

52

value for growing children. Indicated in cases of malnutrition, rachitic conditions, skin complaints — especially when the skin is dry or rough, inability to store fat, poor development of teeth and bones and sensitivity to bright lights. A deficiency hastens senility and reduces the life span. The quantity of vitamin A in milk depends on the nature of the feed available to the animals. When fed on rich, green pasture the vitamin is more abundant, and lessens when the animals are fed on hay and root crops. So to those who say 'eat beef and be as strong as the ox' we reply, what made the ox strong? The answer is sun-saturated grass! Sufferers from high blood pressure and heart or arterial disease should confine their fat intake to the unsaturated fats and oils, and partake of the green vegetables rich in this vitamin.

VITAMIN B. Known as water soluble B this important vitamin is found almost entirely in plant foods, although also present in liver and brewer's yeast, lean meat and fish roes. B is not a single vitamin but consists of a series: B, B1 and, at the time of writing a B12 has been discovered. The latter being of special value in nervous and even certain mental disorders. The B group play a large part in promoting growth and dealing with emaciation. Special names have been given to B vitamins. For example B1 is called Thaimin and B2 Riboflavin; yet another is called Niacin.

Conditions responding to vitamin B are: mental depression, mental laziness, nervous headaches, nervous exhaustion, loss of memory, hypersensitivity to noise, insomnia, swellings of the limbs, digestive disorders, poor appetite, cracked lips, dryness of the skin, loss of hair, trouble with vision, loss of muscle tone etc. It has also found to be of value in lack of muscular co-ordination, anaemia and eczema.

It is interesting to note that bacteria associated with even the most serious disorders increase in numbers in people lacking in the vitamins, especially in B and C. The bacteria grow and multiply to the danger point only in pathological soil. During times of famine when the intake of good food is limited disorders such as tuberculosis manifest in an alarming manner. This proves that a body endowed with pure blood

53

and tissues becomes immune to germ diseases, and that such diseases are not basically caused by germs but by nutritional faults.

VITAMIN C. This vitamin is ascorbic acid and can be produced chemically, although in our opinion the synthetic vitamin seems to lack some of the values of the natural item as provided by plant life. Vitamin C is found in abundance in rose hips, black currants, kale, sprouts and parsley. Also to a lesser extent in oranges, lemons, grapefruits, loganberries, currants, strawberries, cabbage, asparagus, germinated peas, spinach, rhubarb and liver. Additionally it is found in apples, plums, onions, beets, carrots, parsnips, tomatoes, raspberries, beans, lettuce, swedes, potatoes and milk. Recently red pepper was discovered to be a good source.

Rose hips and black currants (in any form) are used extensively for the treatment of colds and the latter has been a favourite country medicine for winter ailments for generations. This vitamin is of great value in the treatment of scurvy and blood disorganisation, low resistance to disease, debility and sinus infection.

Of all the vitamins C seems to be the least stable and most of it is lost by cooking. All the evidence shows that the system requires an amply supply of vitamin C, especially when colds are present. When the natural sources are not available the synthetic tablets may be taken with safety. The timely intake of C at the first sign of a cold is of proven value, but to be really effective massive doses are required. One may take plenty of the indicated fruit juices, blackcurrants or rose hip syrup (or tablets) and the largest dose for rose hips in any form is advisable in such circumstances. Acerola tablets (akin to the rose hip in nature) may be taken instead of rose hips and are an even richer source of this vitamin. One difficulty is the cost of the tablets. So those who are poor in purse may rely on plenty of acid fruit drinks or the extracted juice of rose hips. The old herbal school made much of the value of red (Cayenne) pepper in the treatment of colds, and it now appears that at least some of the value of this article lies in its high content of vitamin C. All wild herbs are vitamin rich, and any herb with alterative (blood cleansing) qualities will provide vitamin C, and most of the other vitamins as well.

In addition to its value for colds and catarrh this vitamin is indicated in rickets, disorders of the bones and teeth, anaemia and pyorrhoea. It is unlikely that children provided with an ample supply of vitamin C will develop tooth decay or suffer from bleeding gums, although the intake of white sugar products must be avoided or strictly limited.

VITAMIN D. This vitamin is largely associated with vitamin A. It seems to help in correcting calcium deficiencies, so is useful for early tooth decay and in rickets. Promotes the growth of healthy bones. It is found in all the foods rich in vitamin A, especially in fish oils. One or two capsules of cod or halibut oil daily (when indicated) will soon make good any vitamin D deficiency. But here again those who partake of natural foods will obtain their supply in normal circumstances without having to resort to fish oils. In the old days cod-liver oil was a household medicine for growing children, and although unpleasant accomplished a great deal of good; no doubt the vitamin D content was the reason.

VITAMIN E. The chief source is the germ of wheat. All are advised to take a helping of wheat germ with the daily breakfast. All cereals contain this vitamin, especially in the germ of the grain. The highly processed breakfast cereals are practically useless from the vitamin standpoint. Also found in green, leafy vegetables, herbs and some vegetable oils.

Vitamin E is of special value in heart disease, arterial disorders, loss of sexual power, circulatory troubles, problems related to the menopause and sterility. When indicated it is usually prescribed in the form of wheat germ oil in capsules. The dose is normally shown on the package and most who suffer from a deficiency of the vitamin are advised to take rather massive doses. One difficulty with oily vitamins is that they tend to upset the digestion of those with weak stomachs and livers, and such should rely more on wheat germ cereal and whole grain products.

VITAMIN K. This is found in liver, green vegetables and animal fats. It is claimed to be of value for those with a tendency to blood clotting, jaundice and in haemorrhages.

VITAMIN P. Found mostly in acid and sub-acid fruits and in rose hips. This vitamin is of pronounced value in cases where the small blood vessels (capillaries) are fragile. Hence it is especially indicated in cases of high blood pressure, haemorrhages and arterial and vein disorders.

Probably the richest source of P is the peel of oranges and lemons. So sufferers from the troubles mentioned may chew some of this peel to advantage every day. Well masticate, swallow some juice and eject the residue. Said to have some value in duodenal ulcers. Vitamin P is found in the juice of these fruits, and in fruit juices generally; also in rose hips.

Little is as yet known about other vitamins, and to discuss them would tend only to confuse the reader.

Based on investigation it would appear that seaweeds, especially kelp (fucus vesiculosus) is rich in all the mineral salts and vitamins, so much so that the matter will be given special attention.

THE SCHROT CURE

Known as the Schrot Cure or the Regeneration Treatment, this method of natural healing was very popular on the Continent many years ago, and is still employed in some leading nature cure health homes. The writer has visited one such establishment in England and witnessed the successful treatment of many deeply-seated disorders. The cure may be the rather strict method used by Schrot himself, or a modified and more simple system. The original system cannot be said to be exactly a pleasant experience for the sufferer; but the results obtained can be really startling.

The idea is to encourage the elimination of pathological (toxic) causes and restore the system's vital force by the withdrawal of food and drink, and especially of the latter. That is why it is sometimes known as the 'dry diet system'. By this method the entire organism, especially the digestive, is rested, morbid deposits are liberated and the entire body cleansed of disease-causing substances. It is an effective method of regeneration and a cure for the so-called incurables.

Toxins are expelled by means of expectoration, perspiration, urine and stool. Effects are not immediate of course, but from the commencement of treatment discomfort dominates the patient, and renders it rather distasteful to many. To be carried out properly it calls for courage and determination and the system is not recommended for sufferers from high blood pressure or arterial disorders. By the partial deprivation of food and drink, the stomach and organs of digestion are forced to dissolve dry food by means of their own secretions, and without the assistance of other liquids. As a result of the want of water, the morbid matter in the body is gradually loosened and eventually eliminated. The employment of certain water packs (hydrotherapy) during the cure speeds up the treatment and hastens results.

Before commencing the actual treatment it is advisable to eat very sparingly for about one week. Drink only when thirsty and omit condiments or anything in the nature of spices which tend to excite the thirst.

The application of a wet body pack every early evening or on retiring is strongly advisable as this is one of the best methods of eliminating toxic matter via the skin. It is, incidently, also a very excellent method of treating colds and fevers of almost every nature, and will make short work of any such illness. Place a waterproof sheet on the bed and on top of this dry towels, and a large blanket. For the very weakly use two or more dry blankets. Wring out a small sheet in either cold or tepid water and lay it over the top blanket. The sufferer is then laid on the wet sheet which should be folded double, and then placed over the sufferer to reach from hips to under the arm pits. Then wrap over the dry blanket or blankets. Place a hot water bottle to the feet and in the case of very weak people additional hot water bottles to the sides.

57

It is suggested that for the weak tepid water be used. The patient will soon become warm and usually starts to perspire after a short time. The pack may remain on for one to three hours, and if administered at night it will not matter if the person being treated goes to sleep and remains in the pack until morning.

If sweating does not take place within half an hour remove the pack and rub the body with warm olive oil. The pack treatment should be tried again after twenty-four hours. It is advisable in most cases for this pack treatment to be continued daily or nightly for the duration of the Schrot treatment in addition to the week previously.

Always administer these packs in a warm room, well ventilated. When it is found impossible to induce sweating a smaller pack may be employed covering the small of the back and abdomen only. When packs are removed they are impregnated with toxic matter and in some cases are even discoloured; so after removal the sheet should be boiled and thoroughly cleansed. Blankets also should be changed after two or three treatments.

The smaller abdominal pack will often prove to be almost as effective as the large body pack, and is excellent for colds, fevers, bowel disorders, kidney weakness, female troubles and toxic conditions.

Following the removal of a pack the body should be sponged over with vinegar or diluted vinegar, except in cases where olive oil has been resorted to. The vinegar application has a tonic and stimulating effect. After a week the actual Schrot treatment may be started.

When a sufferer is really unwell or suffering from some obvious disorder this treatment should only be administered under the advice and supervision of an experienced practitioner, but all may use it safely when employed in a modified form, in which rather more food and liquid may be taken.

The patient has for breakfast and supper a stale wholemeal roll or a rye biscuit, and a small glass of water or good wine.

For those unable to chew properly the roll may be boiled to a thick mass instead of being eaten dry. For the mid-day meal have vegetables boiled down thick, or stale rolls or stale wholemeal bread. A little honey or brown sugar if desired, or boiled whole rice with a sprinkle of nutmeg, or barley gruel, or a large cup of slippery elm food (any brand). Those who have boiled foods may also partake of a dry, stale roll or rye biscuits.

Be sure to have the pack treatment or, if desired, a steam bath instead; but those with high blood pressure or heart disease should avoid steam baths. When very thirsty a very little cold water or wine may be sipped slowly, but only when really necessary. None of the usual beverages. Occasionally, during the strict system, a scrambled egg on toast may be taken for a change. The main consideration is to restrict the intake of food and liquid, especially the latter.

It is a good plan to keep handy some glass jars in which the patient's urine can be kept for about eight hours. When the urine is no longer cloudy and free from sediment this is proof that the treatment has been successful. For comfort about every third day more water or wine may be taken, but be very moderate. The surest sign of recovery is always the appetite with watering of the mouth.

The treatment may be continued for as long as is necessary, although one week is sufficient for most. After the course of treatment the increased intake of both food and liquid should be a gradual process.

There is no doubt that the restriction of food and liquid intake, coupled with pack treatment, cleanses the entire system and does much to eliminate the accumulated toxins responsible for so many disorders. It also results in an increase of energy, and a host of physical troubles tend to disappear such as gastric ailments, flatulence, acidity, rheumatism, herpes, skin disorders, blood disorders, various inflammations, nervous disorders and complaints which have not been correctly diagnosed.

Arguments have taken place as to whether milk is a suitable food for adults, or should be given to infants and children only. No doubt the contentions will continue. We are inclined to the view that milk should not be combined with other foods, apart from fresh fruits, yet there is not the slightest doubt that milk taken on its own is a most desirable food and remedy. As disease can only be cured by and through the blood and its circulation in the system, it follows that any foods that improve the quality and circulation of the blood will assist greatly in disease removal. Evidence proves that milk makes the purest and richest blood possible. Also it is noteworthy that where the blood pressure is too high or too low the pressure becomes normal on the exclusive milk diet. The only other remedial measure called for when on this treatment is a daily warm bath, and when the body is ready plenty of exercise in the fresh air.

Opponents of the milk diet forget that the value of milk has been proved by the acid test of time. Hippocrates advised milk in large quantities for consumptives and all the ancient physicians held a similar opinion. All civilisations in all ages have recommended milk for curative purposes, and many natural healing establishments employ the system in our own time. There is hardly a disorder in which milk administered in the proper manner will not get rid of most disorders, build vitality and restore the sick to vital well-being. It is an indisputable fact that the use of milk in certain diseases produces results obtainable by no other method.

The milk used should be fresh and unpasteurised (no need to have any unfounded fear of germs), and cow's milk is the best for this method. The writer has had actual health home experience, where all patients were placed on the exclusive milk diet, usually following a brief fast. Indeed it is suggested that a short fast of one to three days (or more) before commencing the treatment prepares the system to deal more effectively with the milk intake.

The quantity used is large and may surprise many. Keep in

mind that a baby for its size takes quite a large quantity of milk daily, and the adult body requires a proportionately larger quantity of this fluid, as the water content is a high one.

Milk contains all the salts and vitamins necessary for the building and health of every part of the body. On the treatment ample rest is essential and plenty of fresh air. Every unnecessary drain on the vital resources should be stopped, so sexual activities should be abandoned for the length of the treatment. Incidentally this form of treatment is excellent for impotence and sometimes will produce results unobtainable by other means. The treatment is not advised for any person who has recently been operated on, or who has suffered from a ruptured capillary or artery. To obtain the ideal results the milk must be used as advised and ample rest taken, plus daily warm baths or showers.

Enough milk has to be taken to improve the circulation, create new cells and tissues and produce prompt elimination of body toxins. The quantity advised for most adults is from five to six quarts daily. The milk should be taken in sips, or through a straw, from clean tumblers. Sip a tumblerful every half hour from the time of waking up until retiring at night. Make the intervals between drinks as regular as possible. If the patient falls asleep a tumbler should be taken immediately on awaking. It must be stressed that as milk is a food it must be sipped or taken slowly through a tube. Get the saliva to mix with every sip taken – good results depend very largely on observing the rules. A partial milk diet may be quite useless.

The duration of the treatment may be from one to four weeks, or even longer. Just a few may find it tends to cause constipation at first. This tendency soon passes. However, when the lower bowel is very obstructed the stool may be broken up with the finger (in a finger stall). On rare occasions a dose of castor oil may be necessary, or an enema. No patient should strain at stool. This applies especially to sufferers from piles. During treatment deep, rhythmic breathing and relaxation will be decidedly helpful. On occasions, if the desire persists, a little fresh fruit juice may be taken between milk

61

drinks.

For periods longer than one week those who are in a very depleted condition are advised to take this cure in a nature cure healthatorium.

FOOD ACCESSORIES

LESSON 5

A small book written by the author on the health value of seaweed has had a world-wide circulation. For many years efforts had been made to discover a herb that would supply all the essential mineral salts and vitamins to replace the multitude of expensive compounds and tablets sold in the shops, but so many wild herbs were required and the fact had to be faced that the boiling required to produce the extracts destroyed many of the most essential elements. Also to make and prepare herbs for tea-making was most inconvenient, and people wanted the proposed remedy in tablet form for convenience.

The sale of mineral salts and vitamins has become an expensive commercial racket, and so many who can ill afford to pay for these products do not really require them, for a natural diet will usually supply most of the human necessities. However, so few in these times can obtain truly natural foods, and so much that is sold is contaminated with poisonous sprays and chemicals, that the need for a convenient food supplement to make sure that all the essential salts and vitamins were available was obvious. Eventually we reasoned

63

that as all life started in the waters of our planet the answer probably lay in seaweeds. Exhaustive research, coupled with long experience, resulted in the discovery that the form of seaweed known as Kelp or Bladderwrack (fucus vesiculosus) was the answer, for Kelp contains all the accessory items required, even the important iodine that the human glandular system needs to keep the glands healthy and active.

Kelp may be taken either in tablet form or as a powder sprinkled over any meal. The dose for the average Kelp tablets is one before, after or during every meal of the day. They are better chewed with the food eaten, and taken thus are not unpleasant. Or, half a small teaspoonful of the powdered article may be sprinkled over the food.

In order to show the undoubted value of kelp here is an analysis taken from Northern seas made by the Norwegian Institute of Seaweed Research. It must be pointed out that the analysis of seaweed here presented is the *average*, as seaweeds differ very slightly in chemical composition according to season and the locality from which they are obtained. A problem to be faced is that so many coastal waters today are contaminated with atomic and other waste products, so the seaweed used for human consumption must be gathered from uncontaminated waters. Seaweed gathered from near the outlets of rivers is always suspect and should be avoided. Few foods these days totally escape the effects of pollution in one form or another. It is the price we pay for our so-called civilisation.

ANALYSIS (Average)

COMPONENTS		CARBOHYDRATES	
Proteins	5.7%	Mannitol	4.2%
Fat	7.0%	Alginic Acid	26.7%
Nitrogen-free extract	58.6%	Methylpentosans	7.0%
Moisture	10.7%	Laminarin	9.3%
Ash (minerals)	15.4%	Undefined sugars (natural)	14.4%

ELEMENTS

Element					Value	Element					Value
Silver	-	-	-	-	.000004%	Molybdenum		-	-		.001592%
Aluminium	-	-	-		.193000%	Nitrogen	-	-	-	-	.062400%
Gold	-	-	-	-	.000006%	Sodium	-	-	-	-	4.180000%
Boron	-	-	-	-	.019499%	Nickel		-	-	-	.003500%
Barium	-	-	-		.001276%	Oxygen	-	-	-	-	Undeclared
Carbon	-	-	-		Undeclared	Osmium	-	-	-	-	Trace
Calcium	-	-	-		1.904000%	Phosphorus	-		-	-	.211000%
Chlorine	-	-	-		3.680000%	Lead	-	-	-	-	000005%
Cobalt	-	-	-		.001227%	Sulphur	-	-	-	-	1.564200%
Copper	-	-	-		.000635%	Antimony		-	-	-	.000142%
Fluorine	-	-	-		.032650%	Silicon	-	-	-	-	.164200%
Iron	-	-	-	-	.089560%	Tin	-	-	-	-	.000006%
Germanium	-	-	-		.000005%	Strontium		-	-	-	.074876%
Hydrogen		-	-	-	Undeclared	Tellurium		-	-	-	Trace
Mercury	-	-	-	-	.000190%	Titanium	-	-	-	-	.000012%
Iodine	-	-	-	-	.062400%	Thallium	-	-	-	-	.000293%
Potassium		-	-	-	1.280000%	Vanadium	-	-	-	-	.000531%
Lanthanum	-	-	-		.000019%	Tungsten	-	-	-	-	.000033%
Lithium	-	-	-	-	.000007%	Zinc	-	-	-	-	.003516%
Magnesium	-	-	-		.213000%	Zirconium		-	-	-	.000043%
Manganese		-	-	-	.123500%	Uranium	-	-	-	-	.000004%

OTHER ELEMENTS PRESENT

Bismuth, Beryllium, Niobium, Cadmium, Chromium, Cesium, Gallium, Indium, Iridium, Palladium, Platinum, Cerium, Thorium, Radium, Bromine.

VITAMINS

Riboflavin, Niacin, Choline, Carotin. Other vitamins are also present.

It will be seen from this analysis that Kelp contains the vital mineral salts and vitamins necessary for the attainment and retainment of good health. Hence, if a small quantity of Kelp is taken every day there is no need to pay out money for expensive mineral and vitamin compounds. If you are in doubt concerning your daily supply of these essential food accessories you can rest assured that Kelp is the answer to your problems. So take Kelp and forget about the much advertised items in the chemists. Kelp is not expensive.

The claim has been made that a regular Kelp intake does much to guard the system from the effects of atomic radiation. This has not been proven, but seems to be justified. Obtain plain, uncoated Kelp tablets made from the powder.

65

Coated tablets usually contain the extract, which is not nearly as effective. The natural iodine in Kelp is a thyroid normaliser, helping the thin to put on weight and the stout to reduce. It is of value in emotional states.

PURIFIED BONE MEAL

Deficiency of calcium can lead to rickets, muscular weakness, poor physical development and disorders of the bones and teeth. It is true that most people obtain an ample supply of calcium in the average diet. This is proved by the quantity of calcium voided in the urine, yet people often suffer from a calcium deficiency. The reason is that they do not assimilate calcium. The fault may be due to poor digestive or bowel weakness, but is usually found in poorly functioning parathyroid glands. These small glands, situated round the thyroid, deal with calcium metabolism, and the assimilation and distribution of this mineral depends to a large extent on the normal functioning of these glands. Very often to administer calcium in homoeopathic form, or biochemic tablets (both homoeopathy and Schuessler biochemistry supply elements in potentised form) will correct faulty glandular activity, although iodine and vegetable medicines are sometimes called for.

Purified bone meal is a good source of highly organised calcium and there are very few who will not benefit by taking a little bone meal daily in this form. Moreover, bone meal seems to enable the system to take up the calcium present in other foods. Taken at the same time as Kelp the results are even more pleasing as the two work well together.

Purified bone meal can be obtained in powder or in tablet form from health food stores and some chemists. Those who require calcium are advised to take one tablet with every meal, or sprinkle a little over food, as suggested for Kelp. Most children will benefit by taking one or two bone meal tablets daily whether they exhibit an obvious calcium deficiency or not. Be sure not to take bone meal as supplied for soil treatment; the purified article is essential for human consumption.

Many young people have lost their tendency to sluggish growth, or disorders affecting the bones and teeth, by taking bone meal daily for a lengthy period of time. The product never causes any harm.

BRAN

Natural healers have recognised the value of bran for a very long time. It is not only mineral-rich, it activates the colon and is a natural cure for many cases of constipation. As a rule a breakfast of soaked prunes with a little molasses and a helping of any good bran cereal will deal effectively with most cases of costive bowels.

It must be kept in mind that a host of disorders have their origin in a toxic state of the system, and such toxic states can be traced mainly to an inactive colon. Orthodox doctors recognise this fact and are usually concerned with the bowel activity of their patients. Only recently has the orthodox profession recognised the great value of bran as a colonic activator. Not only does the roughage itself stimulate the bowels naturally, it also helps to absorb toxic waste which is eliminated with the stool. Additionally, vital mineral salts are taken up from the bran and induced into the blood via the minute absorptive organs present in the bowel lining. Hence bran is not only a bowel activator, it is a valuable tonic food, of proven value in cases of general debility and malnutrition.

For generations the value of bran tea has been recognised. A brew made from bran is excellent for deficiency disorders where there is a lack of calcium, iron, sodium, potassium, silica and other mineral salts. Backward children usually thrive on it when taken two or three times daily.

Pour a pint of boiling water over two heaped tablespoonsful of clean wheat bran. Simmer gently for about fifteen minutes, and then strain through a fine sieve. The flavour is improved and the curative virtues increased if a handful of raisins is added before simmering. The dose is a large wineglassful, taken warm for preference, before or after meals two or three times daily. Honey and/or lemon may be added to taste. Suitable for all ages and it does much to build a healthy constitution and ward off colds and catarrh. Improves the digestion.

Bran poultices are of much value in the treatment of malnutrition, rickets etc., and for abdominal complaints. Loosely fill a flannel or linen bag with bran. The size should be sufficient to cover the area to be treated. Pour boiling water over the bag, place in a towel and wring slightly. Apply as soon as it is cool enough for the patient to bear without discomfort. Use over the abdomen nightly, and bind in position (not tightly). This abdominal application is recommended for the complaints already mentioned. To treat sciatica apply to the lower back. The bran pack may also be used for painful joints, or round the neck for throat complaints. Never bind tightly. Keep an abdominal pack on all night. Other packs may be removed after a few hours, and renewed if necessary. Nourishing and curative properties from bran are actually absorbed into the system when a pack is applied.

ROSE HIPS

The value of rose hips as a rich source of vitamin C has already been discussed. The system requires an adequate supply of vitamin C daily, especially when colds, catarrh and chills threaten. Rose hips are both food and medicine, and the average diet is sadly deficient in the vitamin with which the hips are so richly endowed.

The hips are made into either a syrup or in the form of tablets. This valuable food/medicine may be taken at all seasons of the year, especially in changeable weather and in winter. To make good the daily supply of vitamin C the syrup or tablets should be taken at least once daily, but no harm can possibly result if taken two or three times daily — a teaspoonful or more of the syrup at a time, or one or two of the tablets. When colds are threatened or make their appearance the doses can be increased to advantage – even four of the tablets every two hours during the day. The remedy also helps to build vitality and conquer fatigue.

HAWTHORN BERRIES

The ripe fruit of the hawthorn is a wonderful remedy for weak hearts and circulatory disorders. An Irish physician made a fortune (so it is said) by prescribing a secret medicine for heart disorders, and was visited by sufferers from all over the world. After his death the nature of his secret heart medicine was disclosed, and it turned out to be nothing more than a preparation of fresh hawthorn fruits (berries).

Both herbalists and homoeopaths agree that it is the nearest approach to a positive heart tonic that there is, and a perfectly harmless one. It strengthens the muscle and valves of the heart and is of value in all those disorders which tend to accompany heart weakness, such as dropsy, high blood pressure, debility and mental anxiety. To be really effective the medicine must be prepared from the fresh berries. Extracts prepared from the dried berries are not nearly so effective and such preparations are subjected to high temperatures during the manufacture, and this destroys the vitamin content and results also in a loss of much of the mineral content and healing properties. The fresh berry tincture may be obtained from homoeopathic chemists. A few herbalists may be able to supply an extract made from the fresh berries, but this is very uncertain. Some years ago the manufacturers of herbal extracts used to supply a fresh preparation, but it was discontinued; probably for financial reasons. As with rose hips, hawthorn berries may be regarded as a food as well as a medicine. A full investigation as to the chemical and vitamin content has not been made but it seems obvious that the fresh berries are rich in both mineral salts and vitamins.

When there is difficulty in obtaining the fresh preparation the medicine may be made at home without difficulty. Collect ripe, rosy-red berries; lay them between clean linen and crush them with a rolling pin or a flat iron. Three parts fill a glass or earthenware jar with the crushed berries and top up the jar with good quality sherry wine or brandy, although the latter is an expensive item and wine is quite satisfactory. The alcohol content of the wine or brandy is essential to prevent the medicine from turning 'bad'. The wine or brandy extracts the remedial values from the berries and the medicine thus made will keep for a very long time. Give the preparation a thorough stir daily for fourteen days. Then strain through muslin and bottle. Keep in a cool, dry place. The dose is ten to fifteen drops in warm or cold water before or after meals, three times daily. Two or three drops are ample for the very young, but as the medicine is harmless over-dosing is unlikely. Some practitioners advise as much as a teaspoonful three or four times daily, but such massive doses are unnecessary. This is one of the few medicines advised in strong, unpotentised form by the homoeopathic school. The botanic name for the hawthorn is *crataegus oxycantha*.

To produce the best results hawthorn medicine must be taken for some considerable time. The hawthorn is a member of the rose family and most of these have curative effects on the heart and circulation. The dose for the fresh berry tincture as supplied by homoeopathic chemists is the same as that for the home-made preparation.

COD AND HALIBUT OIL

We have seen that vitamin A is essential to the growth of healthy bones and teeth, that it tends to prolong the life span and enables the thin to put on weight. It also increases resistance to infections and tones the skin. For many years the oil from the liver of the cod-fish has been employed for its value in cases of emaciation, colds and poor development, and with marked success. More recently it has been found that the liver of the halibut is an even richer source of vitamin A, although many experts continue to pin their faith in the oil from cod. Either oil may be used when called for. Halibut

70

oil is usually supplied in capsule form, which eliminates the difficulty experienced by so many people, especially the young, of taking the oil owing to its unpleasant taste. Take the doses as suggested on the bottles or cartons.

Those who prefer to take neat cod oil may disguise the flavour by adding a few drops of oil of spearmint or peppermint to the bottle and giving it a good shake. Another method is to mix each dose with two teaspoonsful of malted milk powder and a teaspoonful or so of orange juice. Add half a cupful of hot milk or water and mix very thoroughly, using a hand-operated or electric mixer. Such a preparation helps to ensure the thorough assimilation of the oil and has additional value in that it is excellent for nervous disorders and makes a fine food-beverage.

The late famous Dr. Fernie was a strong advocate of cod oil in the treatment of general debility, respiratory disorders and consumption of the lungs. And the good doctor advocated this oil before the advent of vitamins. Dr. Fernie was a homoeopath who wrote extensively on the employment of herbal simples and 'kitchen medicine'.

CHARCOAL

It may be argued that vegetable charcoal is not a food and is a 'dead' substance. Yet, it is rich in mineral matter and is one of the best known medicines for dealing with stomach and intestinal flatulence. Also, it is totally harmless. It has been proved beyond all doubt that homoeopathically potentised charcoal (carbo vegetabilis) can be a life-saver, as the potentising process liberates the healing force resident in the substance. It is used homoeopathically for imperfect oxidation of the blood, general debility, sensitivity to cold, venous congestions, fevers, air-hunger, certain mental fears, vertigo, haemorrhages, pyorrhoea, blood disorders, indigestion, flatulence, piles, asthma, varicose ulcers and collapse. It has been termed 'the corpse reviver'.

We are concerned with its use in crude form for flatulence

and stomach and intestinal toxaemia. Tablets of vegetable charcoal can be obtained from most chemists, health food stores and herbalists. Those who suffer from these ailments will be afforded great relief by swallowing one or two charcoal tablets before or after meals, or by chewing them with the food. They will not in any way interfere with any other food accessory or with any medicines one may be taking.

Another way of taking charcoal is in the form of charcoal biscuits. Two or more may be taken with any meal, and they are quite pleasant. Obtain from the same sources supplying charcoal tablets. Crude charcoal is not held out as a cure for dyspepsia and flatulence, but it certainly is a great help and brings speedy relief in most cases. As a rule when one masticates thoroughly flatulence will disappear without any form of medicinal aid.

YEAST

Brewer's yeast is a rich source of vitamin B, and is therefore indicated in nervous disorders, loss of appetite, indigestion, bad memory, mental depression, weak vision, hypersensitivity and poor muscular co-ordination. All nervous functions are helped by this vitamin and it is also beneficial in some skin disorders.

Yeast seems to assist in the assimilation of other foods, and is recommended for all the disorders mentioned. Do not obtain yeast with minerals, but the plain yeast tablets. Take one or two with every meal. Obtainable from chemists, health food stores and herbalists. Will not interfere with other food accessories or indicated medicines.

HONEY

Pure honey is by far the best sweetening agent available and should when possible replace white sugar in beverages. It contains measurable traces of several important minerals, including copper, iron and manganese.

Its constant use aids the functional activities of the bowels and kidneys, and has a very soothing effect upon all mucous surfaces. Given in hot milk or in diluted lemon juice it is excellent for sore throats, colds, coughs and bronchitis. Locally it may be used as an ointment for most sores, wounds and ulcerations. Good for chapped hands and frost-bite, and will do much to reduce swellings both internally and externally. A drop of liquid honey in an inflamed eye will usually give prompt relief, and honey blended with fresh cream is said to be an excellent skin lotion and is recommended for freckles. Spread on clean cloth it is good for sore patches on the skin and for skin irritation. Applied regularly to the anus it is soothing and helpful for 'piles. It has also been found to be of immense value for the treatment of an inflamed or ulcerated cervix of the uterus, and has produced good results when all other means have failed. Apply with the finger two or three times daily, or on a wad of cotton wool pushed into position to contact the cervix.

Said the wise man of old, Solomon: 'My son, eat thou honey, for it is good.' Honey is a good heart food and strengthens that vital organ. A cup of hot water with a good teaspoonful of pure honey gives immediate energy and is superior to the much-advertised glucose. A little lemon juice and a sprinkle of red pepper adds to its energising properties.

A few people do not care for honey taken raw. They should try boiling a teaspoonful or more in water or milk. Boiling does not appear to destroy the healing properties, and boiled honey is most agreeable.

Honey is a rich source of natural sugars and provides instant and long-lasting energy. Ideal for athletes as well as for the weakly. To take two teaspoonsful of honey and the juice of half a lemon in hot water before retiring will promote restful sleep.

LIVER

Liver is indicated in all the disorders for which vitamin B is advocated. A little should be taken every week, or daily when indicated. If you do not care to partake of cooked liver, tablets of this food can be obtained from health food shops. There is no doubt that liver is of considerable value.

In spite of all that has been said advocating various food accessory remedies, we say once again that Kelp is a grand source of all the vitamins and essential minerals, so the average person need not take any other special remedial foods unless he or she suffers from any particular disorder for which any one special item is advocated.

BEVERAGES

Most people take far too much ordinary tea and coffee, and it is usually made too strong. A little in moderation is of value and acts as a stimulant, but coffee at night tends to keep one awake. On the other hand a small cup of black coffee after a heavy meal will encourage digestion. Coffee made from the roasted roots of the dandelion is harmless and may replace ordinary coffee and tea. The dandelion is a satisfactory remedy for indigestion and a sluggish liver. The taste is pleasant and not unlike that of ordinary coffee, and we advocate it as a beverage for all. Of course one can obtain caffeine free coffee; yet, for various reasons, dandelion coffee is to be preferred, especially for those with weak stomachs.

Fruit juices, plain or diluted, may replace all other beverages and they are all systemic cleansers. Tomato juice is also excellent. So is pure water, which has a cleansing action on the entire system; but most of the water provided in our time from the kitchen tap is chemicalised and not a satisfactory beverage. When pure spring or well water is available take it for preference. No matter what the scientists say the water supplied by the authorities is not an ideal beverage. As stated previously wine is satisfactory in moderation, and so is the occasional glass of beer or stout. Spirits should be avoided except for remedial purposes.

Take beverages when thirsty. It is not good to drink any-thing as a matter of habit. But this does not mean that on festive occasions a little wine should not be taken. Merely be moderate.

Other recommended beverages are mint or other herbal teas. These are prepared in the same manner as one prepares ordinary tea – in a teapot, but not one made of aluminium.

The strength of the brew depends on one's taste. May be flavoured with honey, lemon etc. A tea made with common dry garden sage is pleasing to many. It is highly prized by the Chinese who, it is said, cannot understand why we import their own tea and ignore the sage which grows in our country. Sage has been used for generations as a remedy for sore throats, colds, insomnia, and headaches, especially those of the nervous variety. Sage aids digestion.

It usually takes a little time to acquire a taste for herbal teas. Few people really enjoy their first cup of ordinary tea, and unless disguised with sugar, milk or lemon it is in fact a bitter and most unpleasant beverage. Many enjoy Maté tea and this is more healthful than the ordinary. To add a piece of lemon or orange peel to any form of tea provides a trace of the important vitamin P.

PHYSICAL AIDS TO PROMOTE DIGESTION

LESSON 6

Health is not just partaking of wholesome, natural food. It is one thing to eat what is ideally nutritional and another to assimilate the full values of what has been eaten. Oxygen, for example is vital to the adequate nutrition and vitality of the human organism, and as already mentioned, iron is one of the chief oxygen carriers, although the body can only make use of iron as supplied by the vegetable and animal kingdoms, or properly triturated homoeopathically. Crude iron that has not been naturally associated with organic compounds is not assimilated and can even cause harm and eventually produce the very disorders for which orthodoxy advocates it. For example: iron preparations are given for anaemia, but it does not take very long for the digestive organs to be coated with iron rust and render proper digestion impossible, thus leading to imperfect nutrition and making recovery from anaemia impossible.

However, the iron in food cannot carry oxygen throughout the body adequately if the oxygen required is in short supply. Also, if poisonous gases are present in the lungs, the iron molecules can take up poisons present which results in a form of toxaemia. So it follows that the lungs should be clean and, through the correct function of breathing, a constant supply of really fresh air made available.

Although our food creates heat and some energy the gas which actually activates and drives the human machine is oxygen. One can manage very well going without food for up to a period of weeks; water is required more frequently, but for how long can we manage without air? Just for a matter of a minute or so — hence the obvious vital importance of air. Following an accident or a state of collapse, what is the doctor's first concern? Surely it is to apply the oxygen mask to supply the body with an ample supply of this important gas.

Our lungs are of the right size to accommodate the body in which they are situated, and they are there to be used properly. Investigation shows that few civilised people employ the whole of their lung capacity in the function of breathing; the usual being about one-third only. What does this mean? It implies that only about one-third of the waste, toxic gases are exhaled and a similar inadequate quantity of oxygen taken in with every inhalation. Such shallow breathing is bound to result in two things: 1. The blood is never cleared of toxic substances by correct out-breathing, and 2. the system is never supplied with the necessary amount of oxygen; so oxygen starvation results and, of course, nutritional disorders. Peoples who live closer to nature breath much more deeply and evenly than do those existing in the more cultured orders.

The lungs are not designed to exhale all the air present, and there is always residual air; but in shallow breathers this residual air becomes very stagnant and toxic. It will be noted that all great men and women possess rather wide nostrils and are naturally deep breathers. With the weakly it is the reverse. It may be said that the degree of vitality, both mental and physical, depends very largely on the adequate intake of pure air and the exhalation of toxic gases.

'God breathed into his nostrils the breath of life (lives); and man became a living soul'. (Genesis 2:7). 'His breath

77

goeth forth, he returneth to the earth; in that very day his thoughts perish'. (Psalm 146:4). Yes, breathing is the very first and last act of living. No machine can function without the necessary fuel, and as we have pointed out, air is the gas that drives the human engine.

Moreover, there is an extra 'essence' in this breath of life that seems to contain a special life-promoting quality. It is doubtful if this extra something will ever be determined chemically, but its presence is known and has been for thousands of years. The ancients called it 'prana' or 'galama', and that is one reason why breathing exercises form part of the spiritual training of many Eastern peoples.

There is another very important effect of proper breathing. The organs of the chest and abdomen are separated by a muscular partition called the diaphragm. When the function of breathing is performed correctly this particular muscle undergoes an up-and-down movement, and this provides an internal massage to the organs of digestion — a natural exercise which does much to keep them active and healthy. Thus it will be seen that proper breathing is bound to assist the functions of digestion and assimilation, with the good results one would expect.

Some experts have said that oxygen is the chief brain food, and it has been noticed that backward children commence to make real progress at school when they perform breathing exercises daily. A better oxygen supply to the brain wakes up the brain cells and makes thinking easier and concentration better. Deep, rhythmic breathing will activate the brain, restore vitality, promote nutrition and lengthen the life span. No matter how one feeds, the importance of a normal supply of pure air is vital if real good is to result from attention to proper dieting. Air is one of the few things not taxed by the government, and we are inclined to ignore the fact that it is free and present for our constant use. True, our air is being polluted daily by chemical fumes and the discharges from factories; so it is wise when possible to get away from the towns and take in the purer air of the country. Mountain air is especially invigorating. The circulation of the blood benefits considerably from proper breathing. Air should reach the skin as well as being drawn into the lungs. That is why it has been found that arctic explorers use widemesh underwear, as they keep warmer when the air can get to the skin.

A young fellow taking part in a carnival was covered from head to feet with gold leaf. After a short time he collapsed and died. The investigation revealed that he had died from suffocation. What happened was that the gold leaf had totally obstructed his skin so that he could not excrete toxins via that organ nor take in any oxygen. There is every evidence to show that the skin is a wonderful organ of both secretion and excretion and much more than a garment of protection. To be healthy the skin must breathe, and that is why daily friction baths are very helpful in promoting well-being. The kidneys and the skin are closely associated and when there is kidney trouble the skin takes on part of the work normally performed by the kidneys and throws off additional toxic matter.

There is never any need to strain when performing breathing exercises. Air capacity will gradually improve with practice, as also will nutrition and vitality. The work performed by the diaphragm when correct breathing is practiced will be a positive aid to the function of the stomach, duodenum, liver and pancreas, and prove to be a positive aid to normal assimilation and nutrition.

BREATHING EXERCISES

To get the best results from deep, rhythmic breathing it is essential to adopt the correct posture. It is useless performing breathing exercises if the body is bent forwards or the chest sunken in. The human being was intended to be upright. This is an argument against the use of unsightly high-heeled footwear as they force the wearer to adopt an unnatural posture which throws the spine out of position. Many troubles due to spinal faults can be traced to high heels.

Sit or stand with the shoulders held back. This extends the chest wall. It will be helpful if a walking stick is placed between the bends of the elbows and the stick held against the back; this extends the chest. To be truly effective all movement when breathing should be confined to the abdomen. That is to say the diaphragm is employed when exercises are taken, the importance of which has already been discussed.

1 PREPARATORY AND CLEANSING BREATH

After adopting the correct position take a few deep breaths, in and out *through the mouth,* at about the same rate as one employs when using a saw for sawing wood. Do this for six to twelve times. Keep the chin in when breathing. Apart from this first preparatory breath all breathing should be *nasal.*

2 TO ELIMINATE TOXINS

After performing the preparatory breathing take in a full breath through the nose and allow the air to be expelled slowly until you cannot breath out any more without undue strain. Pause, holding the breath for a few seconds, and then inhale with a full breath. Repeat this for six to twelve times once or twice daily. When possible perform all the exercises in the open air, or in a well-ventilated room.

3 TO INCREASE VITALITY

Exhale fully and then slowly inhale to fill the lungs to the fullest possible extent. Hold the inhaled breath for a few seconds and exhale deeply and thoroughly. Repeat six to twelve times. This exercise helps to charge the system with energy while No. 2 gets rid of toxic gases. As a poet has expressed it: 'Every inhaled breathe brings life; exhalation breathes out strife.'

4 GENERAL DEEP BREATHING

When sitting or standing in the correct posture breathe regularly, in and out through the nose for several minutes. The ideal time is seven seconds for the inhalation and seven for the exhalation. Pause for one second between each in and out breath. Many will be unable to attain the rhythm of seven seconds at first, but the time will lengthen by constant practice. Some may manage only four or five seconds at first until the lungs improve through constant exercise. This exercise may also be taken when out walking, counting to the rhythm of the steps: up to seven for the inhalation, pause for one step, then seven for the exhalation followed by a one step breathing pause, and so on. This is strongly advocated whenever you are out taking a walk.

Thorough exhalation is more difficult than inhalation, and many who cannot take in a really deep breath should concentrate on improving their exhalations. The lungs are like rubber bulbs: when they are squeezed empty they refill automatically. As a rule when the exhalations are complete inhalations look after themselves.

5   ANOTHER EXERCISE

Perform exercise No. 1. Fill the lungs thoroughly and then exhale slowly as you walk up the stairs. Pause when the lungs are empty, take a deep breath and repeat breathing out fully and then slowly inhaling. This is a good exercise for those with weak hearts, but sufferers must never strain. Performed gently this exercise strengthens the heart muscle and promotes the circulation.

Beyond air, light, food, water and exercise we should need no other remedies, always provided that the thinking is positive.

RELAXATION

It has been said that work never killed anybody. Yet a tired mind and body needs ample rest. Early to bed and early to rise is an old and proven slogan, but the trouble is that most people never rest properly as they cannot relax. Also, digestive and other physical upsets tend to render real rest almost impossible. Many cannot sleep at night owing to an over-active mind. Perfect relaxation is essential to refreshing sleep, and enables the system to recuperate. Digestion and assimilation are encouraged by a short rest after any heavy meal and real healing takes place only in a relaxed organism. Nervous tension (inability to relax) is a modern disease, and scores of people rely on suppressive drugs in order to sleep. And the more they take the more they become dependent on such drugs.

Relaxation has been included in this course on nutrition as a relaxed body is so essential to proper digestion and assimilation. And so is a peaceful mind, for the state of the body reflects the state of the mind, and vice versa. So it follows that any means of relaxing the mind will help to relax the body. Likewise, physical attention to the body to produce relaxation of the organs will have a beneficial effect on the mind.

Unhappiness, fatigue and many physical disorders indicating a lack of ease (dis-ease), are associated with tension. Headaches, nervous disorders, digestive trouble, acidity, constipation and many complains are associated with the inability to relax. The hurry of our modern age does not help people to relax and many means can be taken to induce relaxation. It must be stressed that careful dieting will have little or no good effect if it enters a tensed-up organism, for in such circumstances the food eaten can do very little good, and may even set up a toxic condition. Of course the wrong food will cause even more harm. Life is so often a rush affair and a fever of excitement.

The method of relaxation devised by the late L. E. Eeman has proved to be an effective aid in producing a relaxed mind and body, and is excellent for insomnia, for the latter disorder can be due to an over-active mind, or to digestive upsets. The breathing exercises will also do much to calm the mind and induce restful sleep, and such exercises should precede the Eeman treatment as a preparatory treatment. Mr. Eeman's system is based on the fact that the body is a collective mass of electrically charged cells, and every cell has a positive and a negative pole. Some body cells are electrically positive and others are more negative. Health demands a condition of polarisation in which the flow of positive and negative energy is normal. In disease states some organs are too positive and others too negative. This is borne out in the ancient Chinese Acupuncture with its system of meridians or channels of energy.

The subject lies down on a couch or in bed and wills himself to let go in mind and in body. Imagine yourself to be sinking into the couch or bed and collapsing like an old sock. Link the fingers lightly over the upper part of the abdomen, and cross the feet at the ankles — right ankle over left, or vice versa. Do not permit the fingers to grip or be tense. It is interesting to note that the head is electrically positive and the feet are negative. The right hand is more positive; the left is more negative. The same with the lower limbs, the right being positive and the left negative. When opposite poles are linked there is a free flow of energy throughout the system. Keep totally still and breath deeply and gently. Think only of peace, health and rest. Visualise beautiful scenery, memories of a pleasant holiday away from crowds, a pleasing painting, incidents of your life. The musically-minded can go over restful and beautiful compositions. Here we may add that the Barcarolle from The Tales of Hoffmann has been employed therapeutically in mental homes, and with marked success.

Performed in bed at night this will aid the digestive processes and bring ease to the abdominal organs, as well as bringing peace to the mind and inducing sleep. Indeed, many habitual sufferers from insomnia go off to sleep while in the Eeman position. The originator claims that this position, called 'the Eeman circuit', helps to polarise the system and correct the flow of body electricity. Be that as it may, the system does produce relaxation and is beneficial to both mind and body.

Another method, best taken in the Eeman position (although this is not essential), is to will that your limbs and organs shall be totally relaxed. Address the limbs and organs mentally — talk to them. Commence with the legs and say to them: 'You have served me faithfully and well and deserve rest, so be at peace'. Then visualise the legs as being totally relaxed. Then do the same with the right arm and then the left. Then confine the thoughts to the abdomen and will that the organs in that region be totally relaxed, and say to the stomach, spleen, pancreas, liver and bowels: 'You have performed your services throughout the day and deserve real rest, so be at peace'. Concentrate mainly on any one organ that happens to be out of order and visualise peace and energy flowing into it. Thoughts are very powerful forces. Then confine the thoughts to the chest and its organs: heart, lungs, bronchial tubes. Then to the throat, concentrating especially on relaxing the thyroid gland. Lastly dwell on the brain. Visualising all organs and limbs sinking into a state of absolute repose, thinking of their faithful services and blessing them with your good thoughts.

Another way in which relaxation can be brought about is by making a habit of reading slowly. Many read far too rapidly and this causes tension. Slow reading has helped so many — try it!

INSOMNIA

Dieting and other suggestions given in these lessons will accomplish much to induce restful sleep, especially the Eeman system of relaxation. If you wake up during the night then do so thoroughly. Get out of bed, walk round the bedroom, get back into bed and again perform the Eeman exercise.

Deep breathing and a short, sharp walk before bed will prove to be helpful. Also a hot foot bath before retiring, as this helps to draw the blood downwards from the head and equalise the circulation.

One reason for insomnia is the fear of not being able to sleep. Any anxiety will excite the brain and keep sleep away. A happy, peaceful mind, free from morbid thoughts invites restful sleep. Yet another helpful practice to induce sleep is to let go and review the events of the day backwards. Think backwards from the moment of getting into bed right through to the early events of the morning. Although not essential, this thinking exercise is best undertaken when in the Eeman circuit.

Avoid coffee after tea time, and supper should be avoided

in most cases, although a cup of dandelion coffee, 'Vecon', malted milk or milk alone seems to help some to sleep better. Others find a slice of raw onion beneficial. Not all people can manage to take onions and each must find out what suits best by trial and error. Half a teaspoonful of the tincture of fluid extract of passion flower (passiflora) will help in bad cases. Take in hot water.

CONSTIPATION

Usually a laxative breakfast of soaked prunes with a little molasses and bran cereal will soon get rid of the constipation habit. It must be remembered that the frequency of bowel movement differs considerably with different constitutions, and what is normal for one may not be so for another. It is quite natural for some to have just one motion daily. Others may have two or more; then again there are some who are quite healthy who have a bowel movement every other day.

Keep in mind that many sufferers from constipation have constipated minds. That is to say they are so tensed up and tight in mind that the condition is passed on to the bowels. The function of the brain is to absorb good mental food and eliminate what is bad and harmful. The bowels assimilate and excrete physical nourishment and pathological matter in a similar manner. The solar plexus is located here and has been termed 'the abdominal brain'.

The ancients and several of the old herbal schools of medicine paid much attention to what they called 'the laws of correspondencies', and this law certainly applies to the brain and the intestines. In fact both look rather alike when placed side by side. This law is associated with the 'doctrine of signatures'. It was thought that God had set a signature on plants so that human beings would know how to employ them in ill-health because of their shape and colour. In our scientific age this may sound like a fairy tale, but it happens to be true. Take colour for example: plants with blue (sedative) colours such as the scullcap and valerian were regarded as being good for brain and nervous complaints. Such plants with blue flowers are rich in the mineral salts that tone and build the brain and nerve cells. Plants with yellow flowers, such as the chelidonium, dandelion and berberis were consider good for liver and gall troubles (the bile being dark yellow and the disorder of jaundice produces a yellow skin). Analysis shows that such plants are rich in the elements that activate and normalise the liver and gall bladder, being rich in the sodium salts. Plants with red flowers and fruits assist the heart and circulation, red being the colour of the blood. We think of red clover, the red bark of the sassafras and the wonderful hawthorn berry as being wonderful remedies for blood disorders and weak hearts. These plants are rich in the necessary iron and other minerals.

When it comes to shape think of the scullcap which, as the name implies, is shaped like a human skull, and is excellent for complaints in the head. The leaves of St. John's Wort are shaped like the lungs and are dotted with red spots, suggesting bleeding. This plant is good for lung troubles and haemorrhages. The leaves of the male fern suggest the tape worm and for this parasite there is no better remedy. Plants with small roots like little tubes, such as couch grass, suggest the urinary passages and fallopian tubes. We know that they are excellent for trouble affecting these passages. Scores of such examples could be quoted.

Sufferers from constipation, stomach, liver and gall troubles should avoid cooked animal fats and fried foods until they are well. As a salad dressing use maize or sunflower seed oil with lemon juice added. Yet again we stress thorough mastication.

EXERCISE

Anything that does not breathe or move is dead, for life is movement. The body and its organs consist of muscles and all muscles should be exercised, or they deteriorate and wither. The life of an organism is in the blood and without exercise the circulation becomes sluggish, everything slows up, oxygen starvation takes place and the body becomes toxic and diseased.

Daily exercise helps all organic functions, including that of digestion and assimilation. The importance of breathing has already been discussed. Now we have to deal with exercises that strengthen the stomach and digestion and stimulate the abdominal organs in general. The real value of sane dieting depends very largely on the body being in subjection to the mind, and as common sense tells us that exercise is essential to health, then the mind must be in command and a few minutes devoted every day to curative, health-giving exercises.

A fine exercise to start with is merely stretching. All the animals stretch every so often. Watch your cat at home! Hold your hands by your sides and throw out the fingers to stretch them, using some force. Do this six to twelve times. Then throw out your feet in a kicking motion for a similar length of time.

Stand with your face to the wall; rise on your toes and as you do so stretch up with your right arm, fingers extended, and reach up as far as the fingers will extend, making a real effort. Do the same with the left hand. Repeat six to twelve times.

Stand erect with the head high and the chest extended. Raise the hands over the head and bend down and try to touch the toes. Bring the arms up and repeat six to twelve times. It is important not to bend the knees. Do not strain.

Stand firmly with the feet slightly apart and arms over the head. Turn to the right from the hips. Bend the body downwards from the hips for as far as possible without moving the feet. Repeat as above with the left side. This exercise to be taken alternatively with the right and left sides, six to twelve times.

Stand erect with the arms held shoulder high, keeping the hands limp. Swing the body vigorously from side to side while keeping the arms fully extended. Repeat six to twelve times.

Stand or sit in the erect position, keeping the chin in. Imagine you have a large pencil attached to the top of your head and that you are going to describe a circle on the ceiling. Make the imaginary circle as large as possible. There is no need to move the head vigorously, but make the movement with the neck muscles held loosely. Turn the head to the right a few times and then to the left. If you hear some creaking that is a reason why this exercise will do good.

Hold the hands on the hips and swing the entire trunk from the hips with the imaginary pencil still attached to the head, making as wide a circle as possible, to the right for a few turns and then to the left.

For those who cannot perform these exercises very well a short, sharp walk will provide the necessary exercise. Perform the walking-breathing exercise when you take a walk. Walking is a truly effective natural exercise, especially in these times when walking is so rarely indulged in.

For those who are young and well enough most sports are beneficial, and those who engage in the more vigorous sports may not find these additional exercises necessary. Whether you are a sporty type or not, full attention should be given to correct breathing.

Perhaps you have observed the lady 'belly-dancers'. We understand that this form of abdominal exercise is so beneficial that it is difficult to tell the difference between mother and daughter. The exercise results in better digestion and nutrition and it is said that the dancers are never constipated. The exercise makes for a long life and youthfulness. The movement consists of using the abdominal muscles clockwise – up the right side, across to the left, down that side, and repeat, The experienced do this at an incredible speed, but it will help if this exercise (putting the mind into the muscles) is done in moderation. Exercise the muscles in the manner suggested for this is the same course taken by the food residue as it passes through the colon – clockwise.

THE MENTAL FACTOR

LESSON 7

When dealing with nutrition we have to consider mental 'food' as well as physical. Over the years we have contacted many who have dieted wisely, but who still suffer from physical upsets due entirely to a wrong or negative mental attitude. The mind governs the body and its organic activities, so it is logical that the mind must be normalised if we are to have a perfectly functioning organism. To repeat the old saying, 'As we think, so we are'; the entire individual being the sum total of his or her habit of thought and daily activities.

Today a great deal is talked and written about freedom. Human beings love to feel free, but do not understand what real freedom means. Indeed, some obtain satisfaction by restricting the freedom of others, such as authoritative institutions – religious, political and medical. Such institutions greatly restrict the freedom of their own members and place barriers before those outside their own particular fences.

Many people consider freedom to consist of being able to do exactly what one likes whether it be good or bad. This is the freedom of 'conditioned' minds, and can lead to disaster. History proves this to be so, and the lessons of the past show that freedom has to be based on ethics or it becomes an illusion. Human beings are so constituted that real progress cannot be achieved unless thought and action are based on rules of conduct, which really means freedom to do good. In other words freedom lies in being governed by principle and based on universal love. St. Paul informs us that love is the greatest of all attainments; not selfish love, but love that is the perfect expression of unselfishness. Few attain these heights. It is noteworthy that the one who was the friend of the publicans and sinners had some harsh things to say to the religious leaders of his time, calling them 'whited sepulchres' — hypocrites. He quickly forgave the sinful woman and reprimanded those who wanted to stone her to death. It may be said that one reason for the decline of orthodox Christianity is the hipocrisy found in various churches; those who have a 'form of godliness'. The real meaning of Christianity seems to have escaped those who say in their hearts, 'Thank God I am not as other men', when they should be thinking, 'There, but for the grace of God, go I'.

We are agents of free will and the choice as to whether we do right or wrong rests with each of us individually. As everything in nature is governed by law, genuine freedom can only be experienced when these laws are obeyed. Unfortunately the laws imposed by human society are not always based on the rights of the individual, and so often they are unjust and tend to rob people of the necessary human dignity. Hence free will is hampered in the everyday affairs of life. When authoritative institutions say 'thou shalt not' it is sometimes impossible to do good in this world according to the dictates of heart and mind.

We are dual creatures with a free will that enables us to engage in what is good or evil and this struggle between good and bad has gone on since the dawn of time.

Always it is a case of some authority telling us what we may and may not do. As an example, take the authoritative role played by the orthodox medical organisations. People tend to believe that they are always right as doctors have been *trained* in the art and science of healing. People believed in orthodox medicine even when, not so very long ago, they bled people to death for a large variety of diseases. Doctors know that this was wrong and have changed their views. Now blood is given all too liberally for a number of disorders. They may again change their minds, but always what they say is right. There is one matter in which all through the ages medical opinion has been correct until the advent of Freud and his doctrine of freedom and liberation. We refer to the effects of masturbation. Loss of sexual fluids has always been regarded as being detrimental to health and vigour. Freud preached liberation and sexual freedom. The doctors fell into line and sexual freedom has resulted in a frightening state of affairs, for it is always so easy to do what is instinctively wrong when it has the sanction and blessing of authority.

We entirely agree that many sick people in the past who have made a habit of masturbation have been made worse by the fear induced by medical people, priests and others who have informed these souls that they are making a ruin of their health by the habit. The fear of the bad effects and the sin-consciousness has had really bad effects. This goes without question. Now the pendulum has swung the other way and people are even encouraged to masturbate in order to 'liberate' themselves. One very debilitated young man informed the writer that his doctor had advised him to masturbate. Instinctively he knew that this was wrong; but, he reasoned, the doctor must be right. Indulgence in the habit resulted in a gradual decline in his mental and physical health, and we had much difficulty in restoring him. However, there is one body of medical men, who have turned to homoeopathy as a therapy, who still hold the view that sexual expression without common sense can be very harmful. Their remedial measures are calculated to restore the system to a state of normality — not by frightening the sufferer but by re-conditioning him in mind and in body. Homoeopaths, naturopaths and herbalists know the harm that fear installs, but they are also well aware that the loss of vital fluids can result in marked debility and a host of other disorders.

91

The followers of Freud did not always agree about his over-stress about sexual freedom. The creative urge has expression on planes other than the physical, particularly on the intellectual and spiritual levels. We refer to men like Adler, who stressed 'the will to power', and to Jung who paid attention to the spiritual aspect and classified people into two main groups: the introverts and the extroverts. Many of the more modern mental analysts combine what they consider to be the best in the teaching of all three leaders in the field of mental adjustment. Such is human nature that we still find too marked a stress is placed on the sexual side. No doubt the negative part of human nature is relieved by the knowledge that the sins of the past were in fact quite normal. The brake now being off they feel that it is quite in order for them to indulge in every form of morbid sexuality. Anything that savours of true spirituality or of God is regarded as being unnatural and the province of the weak-minded.

We have to thank the evolution theory for much of the moral depravity existing today, and remember it is only a theory. Evolution has not been proven; in fact everything, scientific and logical, goes to show that evolution is a myth. Scientists go on searching for the missing link between man and the apes. This link has never been found and never will be. Is it not logical to conclude that the earth's strata would abound with evidence to show such a link? On the contrary it has been found that fossils of fish and animals that lived thousands or even millions of years ago, to be identical with the skeletons of living creatures existing today. Of course there are many varieties of dogs, horses, fish and other creatures; but they do not change with the passing of time, although they tend to adapt themselves to their environments. Evolution is full of 'ifs', 'buts' and 'surmises'. All the evidence available demonstrates that the various forms of life have been fixed, 'each after its own kind'. A dog is always a dog, a cat a cat and a horse a horse. Man's attempt to produce a different species of animal, such as a mule, is frustrated by natural law, for a mule cannot reproduce. Even man-created flowers tend to revert to the original in course of time. So why is evolution

92

taught as a proven theory in schools and colleges? This is something of a mystery. But it is not the purpose of these lessons in nutrition to deal with such subjects, only in so far as they concern the sort of food that is supplied for mental nourishment. We will close the reference to evolution by quoting from 'The Watch Tower' magazine, January 15th, 1977.

A New York educator recently wrote to 'Science News' magazine of his frustration because graduate zoology students would not think about the 'why' of evolution. 'Though I spent nearly an hour trying, in various ways, to get them to consider the content of the question,' he writes, 'they refused unanimously to answer it, saying that the word "why" brought in teleology [the study of evidences of design (implying God) in nature].'

Though this instructor himself believes in evolution, he complains: 'The word "why" had simply evoked the concept of teleology in a manner which prevented further thinking about the matter. I question the value of scientific schooling that produces such rigid associations between terms and concepts. Is it really necessary? May it not do more harm than good by curbing creative thought on scientific problems?'

Hence, students of science are often taught to close their minds tightly on this fundamental issue. Their thinking becomes as futile as that of ancient pagans described in the Bible: 'Ever since the creation of the world [God's] invisible nature . . . has been clearly perceived in the things that have been made. So they are without excuse; . . . they became futile in their thinking and their senseless minds were darkened.' — Rom. 1:20, 21, Revised Standard Version.

Dispose of God and get rid of ethics and what is the result? The sort of crime-ridden society we have with us today. And things will become worse with the passing of time. The advent of the contraceptive pill has been considered a blessing to many; yet, let us face it, it is another contribution of medical science leading to the freedom to do anything that eventually leads to racial destruction. One wonders what is happening to self-control, real love and true comradeship. The pill does not prevent venereal disease, which is on the increase and is presenting a headache to doctors who just do not know how to deal with the problem. It would be a good idea if an effort were made to forge passion into power. There is some evidence to prove that the pill has long term side-effects that are harmful.

A small book entitled *Medical Nemesis* has been written by Ivan Illich, a noted scholar and research worker. Illich shows in his book that the claims of medicine to have wiped out scourges such as tuberculosis, diphtheria, typhoid, etc., is false. When the new drugs and antibiotics were discovered these serious diseases had already practically vanished. No doubt improved nutrition and a more secure state of living did much to lessen or disperse those disorders. Modern surgery has its place but in most instances surgery is not the answer to peoples troubles, for the cause is always left in the background.

We recall seeing and hearing an American surgeon brought over from the States to exhibit one of his surgical 'cures' of cancer. No doubt bringing the good doctor over to England was a costly business. He appeared on the screen for only a few minutes and pleaded with the public to leave quacks alone and go to a doctor who was properly trained when they had serious diseases, such as cancer. Unfortunately the gentleman 'cured' of cancer by this distinguished surgeon died some months later — from cancer! One notable orthodox doctor has had the courage to state that medicine has destroyed more lives than war, famine and pestilence combined. In our opinion this statement is too sweeping. We cannot manage at present without doctors, but oh that more of them would be like the famous Dr. Aschner who saw the good in most therapies, both old and new, and gave credit where credit was due.

Everything in life is constantly changing except the law of change. You cannot step in the same river twice, for the river is changing constantly. We also are constantly changing and that change is either for the better or for worse. No cell in our bodies is the same today as it was a week ago. We have to change, and by proper nutrition, both mental and physical, the change can be always for the better.

94

One reason for nervous tension and nervous disorders is to fight against circumstances. You cannot use a saw on sawdust, and what has happened belongs to the past, and is so much sawdust. When even the worst is accepted there is nothing more to fear, but everything to gain, for every morning is a fresh beginning. Dr. Niebuhr a New York professor has a prayer: 'God grant me the serenity

To accept the things I cannot change;

The courage to change the things I can;

The wisdom to know the difference.'

Proper feeding may do much for your stomach or duodenal ulcer, although the real cure is to remove the reason why you have an ulcer eating into the tissues – get rid of what is eating you.

Dr. James Gilkey says that we have to be willing to be ourselves, and a state of unwillingness to be oneself lies at the back of many neuroses and complexes. Nobody is so miserable as he who longs to be somebody other than the person he actually is in mind and body. As Shakespeare said: 'This above all, to thine own self be true'.

Dr. Henry Link says: 'No discovery of modern psychology is, in my opinion, so important as its scientific proof of the necessity of self-sacrifice or discipline to self-realisation and happiness'. Self-mastery is the key to all progress and the greatest victory is that attained over self. Employ freedom to be the boss over the self, and play the game of life according to the rules. The rewards are great!

Although spiritual values are on the decline the number of those who could be helped by a realisation of religious values is vast. We quote the great psychoanalyst Dr. Jung: 'During the past thirty years, people from all the civilised countries of the earth have consulted me, I have treated many hundreds of patients. Among all my patients in the second half of life – that is to say, over thirty-five – there has not been one whose problem in the last resort was not that of finding a religious outlook on life. It is safe to say that every one of them fell ill because he had lost that which the living religions of every age have given to their followers, and none of them has been really healed who did not regain his religious outlook.' That is the finding of one of the greatest minds of our time and is worthy of careful consideration. Dr. Jung was asked on television if he believed in God. The old gentleman replied: 'I do not have to believe, I *know*'. Having to believe suggests some effort, and Dr. Jung did not have to make the effort of believing; he *knew*.

Unfortunately, man has created a god in his (man's) image, and he has produced some rather frightening deities. God is the I *am* — the self-existing one, and he is *love*. 'He that loveth not knoweth not God'. Without free-will we cannot be in the image of the Infinite, and to be in tune with the Divine Life we have to follow the laws which spring from God. Employ free-will, do right and be willing to draw on the source of unlimited power. It is there for the asking.

One of the much neglected rituals of the past is grace before meals. Psychologists agree that this act of appreciation calms the mind and helps to prepare the stomach for the process of digestion. If you find time to say grace the meal is unlikely to be hurried — peace of mind followed by peace of the digestives.

Banish all envy, hate, unforgiveness, strife, hurry and anxiety from heart and mind, for they are all narrow, withering forms of fear; for as we have pointed out previously, fear is our worst enemy. As St. Paul said, we should think on the things that are true, honest, pure, lovely and of good report. He stressed the importance of faith, hope and love, and the greatest of these is love. Psychologists agree that the person dominated by love is never frustrated or miserable.

The person who seeks to serve others is never inhibited and is never annoyed or upset. The mental nourishment of such an individual produces a habit of thought in tune with the infinite, and a body governed by such a mind is likely to function far more normally than one who lives in a state of fear and anxiety.

A poet has written:
'Love is the filling from one's own, anothers cup;
A daily laying down and taking up.

96

A choosing of the rugged path in each new day,
That other feet may tread with ease a smoother way.
Love is not blind, but looks abroad through other eyes,
And asks not 'must I give', but 'may I sacrifice?'
Love hides its grief that other heart and lips may sing,
And burdened walks that other lives may buoyant wing.'

We once had a very sick lady who had tried all manner of treatments without success. After a lengthy talk it was discovered that she had been hurt by the action of a dear friend in the past, and that her illnesses had their genesis at that particular time. She had never forgiven her old friend. It was pointed out that her unforgiveness had set up tensions and disturbances in her system, and that unless she truly forgave she could not expect to be forgiven for her own errors. She had the wisdom to see the logic, forgave her friend and wrote her a letter. Quite soon she was both well and happy. By the act of forgiveness her mind and body had been set free from the grip of a destructive emotion.

In spite of the many restrictions that exist we still have free will to take constructive mental nourishment. Read good literature and thereby improve the mind. And read slowly to take in and digest the information gained. As we have mentioned previously, slow reading is a help towards mental and physical calmness. Much of the literature available is mere trash, although there is no objection to reading the occasional thriller. We know of families who make a habit of reading pages from the Bible or a philosophical work every day, and they confess that this practice has achieved much good.

It will be helpful if you realise that you are not the result of some imaginary cosmic accident but the product of design and purpose. That the Eternal intelligence is slowly reproducing itself in its image and likeness, and that the degree of progress depends on you and on the proper use of your free will. On the television not long ago a learned professor was trying to explain that the universe was the result of what he called 'a wonderful accident'. A boy of twelve turned to his father and asked: 'But something must have been there

for an accident to happen and what caused the accident?'
Children so often manifest more common sense than do the
very learned of our generation.

The misuse of free will has resulted in decline and degeneration. Knowledge has increased, but not wisdom. The first
essential step to true wisdom and knowledge is to get to know
yourself and why you are here; secondly, to weave the
tapestry of life according to the rules. In the long ago one
said: 'Consider the lilies of the field, how they grow. They
toil not, neither do they spin——.' Yes, much can be gained
by observing the processes of nature. The lilies grow beautiful
without any effort of their own. They grow because they
cannot do otherwise. They obey the laws implanted in the
seed from which they came. It is always true that we reap
what we have sown.

Hanging near the writer's bed is a pull-switch for the
electric light. This cord can just be touched with the fingers
but not grasped without difficulty. But if the cord is just
touched with the finger tips it swings away, and then returns
so that it can be held without any difficulty. When you have
a problem that you cannot grasp push it away from you and
your mind will retain the problem and, in most instances,
work out the solutions so that when the matter again crops
up you will be able to grasp and cope with it as with the
light-switch cord. To harbour and dwell on problems and
matters that cannot be changed is to invite tension. Brush
them aside and your wonderful, creative mind will provide
the answer in due time.

The body and its organs cannot be cleared from disorders
when the mind is tied up with fears and cluttered with
problems. Let go and be free! Select your mental nourishment
as wisely as you do your daily food.

A lady came to one of our lectures in natural dietetics
to listen, so she said, with 'a perfectly open mind to what
she was convinced was absolute nonsense.' The lady did not,
of course, have an open mind, but a mind conditioned and
obstructed.

Read the lessons and use your logic. 'Prove all things, and

98

hold fast to that which is good'.

In 'Reader's Digest' for January 1977 there appeared a condensed presentation of a book by Dr. Ronald Glasser. The doctor writes in an entertaining manner and dwells much on the body's ability to heal itself. The presentation ends with the following paragraph:

'There are a growing number of facts available that show plainly that we are as much a part of our own diseases as we are of our health, that we should be able to and indeed can help ourselves. The task of the doctor today is what it has always been, to help the body do what it has learnt so well to do on its own during its unending struggle for survival — to heal itself. For it is the body, not the medicine, that is the hero.'

The title of the book is *The Body is the Hero* (Published by Wm. Collins, Sons & Co. Ltd.).

From the above quote one would imagine that the doctor was a homoeopath, for the statement is in line with the homoeopathic concept. But in his writings he stresses the wonderful accomplishments of orthodox medical science and surgery, including transplants. One wonders why, if the body heals itself, orthodox medicine spends so much time in interfering with the natural processes of nature? If the body is a self-healing mechanism, why not devote every possible attention to enabling the self-healing to do its job, and cease adopting measures that thwart the cellular intelligence of the organism?

ADDITIVES AND PRESERVATIVES

It is becoming increasingly difficult to avoid foods that have not been 'doctored' in some manner with flavourings, colourings and preservatives. A few of these are harmless, but other items employed can be quite harmful. As can be sugar replacements such as saccharine. At the time of writing it has been found that saccharine may be a cause of cancer and the American dietetic authorities have taken steps to ban its use

99

in America. The best sugar replacement is undoubtedly pure honey. The facts are that any chemical concoction is unlikely to have any good effects.

For colouring purposes chlorophyll may be used to produce a green colour, and this is not objectional. But any mineral substance employed to produce green (such as copper) is harmful. Cochineal has been made use of for a very long time to produce pink or red colouring, and this item is not objectionable, although the homoeopaths have found that the excessive employment of this article can cause respiratory, head, heart and urinary troubles. In fact it is used in a potentised form for these very complaints. Red dyes from minerals can be most harmful.

Metaphorically speaking people are being educated to 'eat with their eyes'. If a food looks nice and attractive that seems to be all that matters to many.

The most commonly used preservatives are sodium chloride, borax, boric acid, formaldehyde, nitric acid, saltpeter, some of the sulphates, salicylic acid, benzoic acid, saccharine etc. Sulphur dioxide is commonly used as a preservative in beverages. As far as we have been able to gather this does not have any harmful effects in strict moderation, but the long term effects could be dangerous. Those who employ preservatives and dyes in foods and beverages stress the minuteness of the quantity, but any homoeopath knows that minute quantities of a substance can be really dangerous in the course of time. It also follows that any substance which prevents chemical action outside the body must also interfere with the digestive juices. Preservatives in the proportion of one part to 210 parts of any food cause salivary activity to be suspended entirely for a period of five minutes. Salicylic acid, borax and sulphate of lime will suspend salivary activity for up to sixty minutes, or longer with some people; so the digestive secretions of the stomach must likewise be affected.

Saltpetre is used for salting meats and produces nausea, vomiting and diarrhoa and tends to inflame the urinary passages and mucous membranes. All boric acid preparations create digestive disturbances and salicyclic acid depresses the

100

heart and is an irritant to the urinary organs.

Salts of copper are used to produce a green colour and are frequently added to preserved peas. Sulphur will colour food yellow and act as a preservative. Always the ugly finger of greed can be detected in the effort to make foods and beverages attractive, which deceive the public and lead to poor nutrition and disease.

Saccharine is derived from coal-tar and is a poison. Many foods are treated with saccharine and only a very minute quantity can make foods that have lost their natural sweetness appear to taste fresh and naturally sweet. One part of saccharine to one thousand parts of commercial glucose makes the latter as sweet as cane sugar. Most foods sold in tins (possibly all of them) contain harmful preservatives and/or colouring matter. The so-called 'fruit essences' are often just synthetic mineral concoctions.

Evidence concerning the harmful effects of synthetic colouring and preservatives abounds, and world governments are well aware of this; but all that happens mostly is that the manufacturer has to state on the label that the product contains such and such a preservative, concerning the nature of which the unsuspecting purchaser knows absolutely nothing. Manufacturers of some soft drinks used to state on their labels that their products contained sulphur dioxide. At the time of writing the name of the additive has been omitted and the single word 'preservative' added. And that could mean almost anything that happens to be in accord with the law.

It is wise, as far as is reasonably possible, to avoid foods which are tainted with artificial colouring matter or preservatives, especially foods sold in cans and the soft drinks. Even meat is doctored to make it appear red. Fresh foods as supplied by nature are provided in the form in which they were intended for human and animal consumption. Do not live in a state of perpetual fear if you have to resort to the junk foods on occasions. Feed on natural foods as far as possible and nature will take care of your occasional lapses.

When trouble like an angry cloud darkens any nation one of the usual problems is the threat of famine. In such circumstnaces full nourishment may be obtained from sources not normally considered.

As a boy in the Forest of Dean the writer was fascinated by the many Romany families who resided in their caravans in various places in the Forest. They did not appear to engage in any form of soil cultivation, but lived on what nature provided from the earth, the grassland and the hedges. Soups were made from nettles, sorrel, chickweed, dock, meadowsweet and other wild herbs. The leaves and roots of the dandelion were regarded as highly curative for any type of stomach or liver upset. As all wild herbs are packed with essential mineral salts and vitamins they were a healthy people and we never witnessed illness in their ranks, although of course some of them had an illness on occasions. We never heard of a doctor being called and they seemed to rely entirely on their knowledge of herbs for the treatment of any illness. Indeed, some of the Forresters went secretly to the encampments for advice when suffering from various ailments.

When food is scarce or charges are high dig up every available strip of land: lawns, flower beds, borders etc., and plant nourishing vegetables. When land is not available use boxes or tubs and fill them with soil — virgin when possible.

We knew one family during World War II who had no land and the small available space round their home was concreted. But boxes of soil were placed on all the window ledges and other boxes and tubs were arranged on the concrete court. It was astonishing what this gardenless family grew in these crude containers: potatoes, tomatoes, beans, peas, lettuce, carrots, beet, onions, watercress etc. Moreover, they somehow managed to grow sufficient food during the winter months to supply their daily needs. When circumstances are poor others can copy the example of this family. They also found their efforts brought a certain amount of pleasure and satisfaction, and feelings of self sufficiency.

During the same period of World War II the newspapers reported a man who claimed to live almost entirely on fresh, young grass which he used as a salad and also cooked as greens. The grass was carefully selected and the most tender types employed. He claimed that he kept fit and well on this very primitive diet. After all grass is the main food of many animals, wild and domestic, and they all seem to manage very well on this very simple form of sustenance. The fact is that nobody need starve. Naturally it is important to have the right mental attitude to the problem, for if one thinks that grass or wild herbage is not suitable as a food the body will conform to the nature of the thinking. Always go by what the facts disclose and never be guided by conditioned thinking.

Yet again it is stressed that very thorough chewing will guarantee good digestion and assimilation, and all uncooked raw vegetation demands complete mastication.

The inner bark of the elm tree may be grated up and made into a coarse gruel. This is very nourishing and ideal for weak stomachs.

Comfrey roots and leaves may be eaten raw or cooked. They supply most valuable nourishing qualities and help to keep the entire digestive tract and respiratory system in good order. Comfrey (symphytum) has been used for generations as a curative food and medicine for bronchial troubles, stomach and duodenal ulceration and general debility. Also for the healing of wounds and fractures.

Chickweed is as nourishing, so say some herbalists, as the famous American slippery elm. It may be taken in salads or cooked as a vegetable. The weed forms an excellent application for sore eyes, skin disorders and irritation. May be made into a useful ointment by boiling in any fat or petroleum jelly.

Clover leaves and flowers may be added to all salads when available. The red blossoms are in particular good for blood disorganisation and it is claimed help to keep the system free from malignant conditions.

Dandelion roots or leaves are both healing and nourishing.

Add the fresh leaves to salads. The boiled fresh or dried roots form a healing medicine for indigestion and liver disorders. Good for the bowels. The roasted roots make a pleasing and healthful substitute for ordinary coffee.

Dock leaves (all varieties) have nourishing properties and may be eaten raw or cooked. Medicinally they cleanse the blood and are good for skin disorders, rheumatism, coughs and respiratory disorders. There are few, if any, better applications for insect bites and stings than the leaf of the broad dock bound lightly over the area.

Mints, spearmint and peppermint, aid all digestive processes and help to get rid of flatulence. They form a pleasing addition to all salads. Blended with elder flowers, peppermint is an old and proven remedy for colds and influenza. Does much to eliminate catarrh. Take as a tea: one ounce to every pint of water used; a cup to be taken three or four times daily, hot for preference.

Nasturtium seeds are hot and appetising. Add to salads. Good for digestion and general debility.

Nettles (stinging) are great blood cleansers. They cleanse the arteries and help to reduce high blood pressure. Play a useful role in eliminating acids and toxins from the system, and at the same time are as nourishing as most cooked vegetables. Quite harmless. The gipsy people eat a lot of nettles. Will replace cabbage and the usual greens.

Marshmallow roots and leaves are nourishing, healing and not unpleasant used raw or as a cooked vegetable. The plant has been used for generations as a remedy for digestive and respiratory disorders. The dried roots, ground to a powder, make a satisfactory flour for baking purposes.

Rose hips and hawthorn berries are very rich in vitamin C, so are grand for colds and blood disorders. The hawthorn berry is one of the best general remedies for weak hearts ever discovered, and quite harmless.

Rose petals, violet leaves and flowers and many blossoms may be added to salads. All provide some nourishment and curative virtue. Violet leaves, for example, are grand blood cleansers.

104

Onions have for long been recognised as a remedy for respiratory troubles. They are strongly antiseptic and do much to keep one free from infections of all kinds. For a cough sprinkle brown sugar over sliced onion, or cover with honey. Take up to a tablespoonful of the juice which forms several times during the day. This is also of value for colds and bronchitis. Even to smell a raw onion will sometimes abort a certain type of common cold, and the homoeopaths employ potentised onion for the runny type cold and catarrh.

In addition to their curative value onions are most valuable foods. Those who find cooked onions do not agree with them should try a little raw.

One of the best medicines to prevent infection, ward off colds and fevers and provide gentle stimulation is a mixture of powdered cloves and cinnamon. Equal parts are recommended. A quarter of a small teaspoonful in hot, sweetened water or milk may be taken at any time.